STILL DEADLY

ANCIENT CURES FOR **THE 7 SINS**

EDITED BY ANDREW CAMERON AND BRIAN ROSNER

AQUILA
PRESS

Still Deadly: Ancient cures for the 7 sins
A book by Aquila Press
Published September 2007

Aquila Press
PO Box A287
Sydney South NSW 1235
Australia

National Library of Australia
ISBN 978 1 921137 83 9

Cover design and typesetting by Lankshear Design Pty Ltd.

STILL
DEADLY

ANCIENT CURES FOR THE 7 SINS

EDITED BY ANDREW CAMERON AND BRIAN ROSNER

CONTENTS

CONTRIBUTING AUTHORS

Brian Rosner
teaches New Testament and Ethics at Moore Theological College.

Andrew Cameron
teaches Ethics and Philosophy at Moore Theological College.

Bill Salier
is Vice Principal of Moore Theological College and teaches New Testament.

Richard Gibson
teaches Greek and New Testament at Moore Theological College.

Gordon Preece
is Executive Director of Urban Seed.

Graham Cole
is Professor of Biblical and Systematic Theology at Trinity Evangelical Divinity School.

Peter Jensen
is Archbishop of the Anglican Diocese of Sydney.

DEDICATION

FOR MICHAEL HILL
'Master of Mutual Love'
Moore Theological College
1976–1982 and 1987–2006
Lecturer in Ethics and Vice Principal

STILL DEADLY: A PREFACE

Greed. Lust. Envy. Gluttony. Anger. Pride. Sloth.

Pause and consider this list. When you think of this list, *where are you in your mind's eye?* Where do you go in your imagination when you consider greed, lust, envy, gluttony, anger, pride or sloth? A school? A college? Some workplace? A bad party? A television soapie?

Philosopher Simone Weil once said that 'imaginary evil is romantic and varied; real evil is gloomy, monotonous, barren, boring. Imaginary good is boring; real good is always new, marvellous, intoxicating.'[1] It is like that with these seven: to list them on paper looks provocative. The disturbing movie *Se7en*, while obviously portraying each of the seven as somewhat repulsive, still retains a strangely seductive drawing power. Weil was right: on paper, or on a screen, evil is fascinating.

Indeed the seven deadly sins have come to seem a bit sexy, a bit retro, and not even all that evil. One website remembers the 1993 MTV special where music and television entertainers agreed the seven were not really vices.[2] Another site devoted to the seven notes with ironic detachment, 'you probably commit some of them every day without thinking about the rich tradition of eternal damnation in which you're participating'.[3] The sense that they are quaintly hilarious reflects our culture's relentless drive for new forms of entertainment, and laughter happens when you subject old taboos to new contempt.

In Australia, the seven were even used to market a series of high fat, high sugar ice-cream confections. We begin to see that far from being our enemies, the seven very usefully raise brand awareness because they perfectly trademark our culture's worship of consumption.

Sadly, Weil was also right about the list of opposites: generosity, faithfulness, thankfulness, contentment, gentleness, humility, usefulness. They seem so nauseating and *nice* in comparison. Would you have picked up a book with *them* on the cover?

Evil attracts us. Yet we haven't written this book because we fear the seven deadly sins, or because we think that newfound interest in them somehow represents a threat to Christianity. Nor do we feel the need to get angry about them, as if it is either us or them.

It is simply that they sadden us. For ask yourself, with Simone Weil: who is the 'new, marvellous, intoxicating' person to be with? We don't mean for one or two dinner dates. Who would you prefer to go with for a lifetime?

- The greedy or the generous boss?
- The lustful or the faithful husband?
- The envious or the thankful sister?
- The gluttonous or the contented pastor?
- The angry or the gentle father?
- The proud or the humble friend?
- The slothful or the useful brother?

When you thought about that school, college, workplace or party in response to the seven deadly sins above, we're betting that it was a bleak memory of a place you wanted to get away from. (The only one that was likely to be interesting was the television soapie, and that is sad for different reasons.) Each of the seven deadly sins represents a malfunction. Some good thing, originally given by God to be enjoyed with thanks, has filled someone's horizon. Their desire grips them so intensely that it eats away from within like a cancer, wrecking their relationships because they just don't care for anyone else.

We wrote this book as a 'thank you' to Michael Hill, a teacher at Moore College in Sydney who has helped many of us to see things differently. But we're using a different approach from the way Michael taught us.

Our method will be to watch and talk about people's *habits of action and feeling*. When these are good, we call them 'virtues', but the seven deadly sins are examples of the dark side of virtues, called 'vices'.

But we also like the Bible's angle on how to live, and you won't find a list of seven virtues or vices there. The Bible's way of describing life includes far more than seven virtues or vices. So why consider *seven* deadly sins? It is an artificially reduced version of what humans do wrong.

The task of thinking through life in a complex world is difficult, and 'seven' at least offers a way for frail and forgetful humans to cover their bases. (Of course even seven is a little hard for *us* to remember, but ancient and medieval people, who originated this approach to life, could reel off the seven deadly sins and seven major virtues with ease.)

Why would we attend to seven deadly *sins*, and not perhaps to something more useful, such as the nine virtues—love, joy, peace, patience, kindness, goodness, faithfulness, humility and self-control—that the Bible calls the 'fruit' of God's Holy Spirit (Galatians 5:22)?

We have attended to these seven vices because they offer us a vehicle for examining our desires when they have gone haywire. In 1 John 2:15-17, the apostle John tells of a problem that we all carry behind our eyeballs (in what is elsewhere called 'the heart'). He notices the way people become lost in 'the desires of the flesh, the desires of the eyes', and 'pride in possessions'—which, when you think about it, is a desire for the approval and adulation of others. It is almost as if God has made his world 'too good'. We attach to aspects of it voraciously, intensely, obsessively, and destructively.

We hope then that our attention to the seven deadly sins will offer sober opportunity to assess this malfunction in our emotional world, because until our emotional world begins to be changed (with God's help), we won't be free to enjoy the goods that God dreams of for us.

Never mind for the moment why we settled on the thinkers who will aid us in this quest, except to say that each offers long-lost resources to a society so deeply weird that it thinks it is on to something when it 'rediscovers' and celebrates the sins themselves, rather than the Christian sages who so passionately and caringly argued their hearers toward new and better directions.

So although you've picked up this book because it seemed interesting, we hope that you'll become really, really bored by it. Not by the writers, of course; nearly all of them are terrific, and we're honoured that they joined in. No; we hope you'll become bored witless by the pathetic pointlessness of pride, envy, anger, sloth, greed, gluttony and lust. In fact in almost every way, it is entirely inappropriate to organise a book about the seven deadly sins; and we hope you'll lose interest in them when you see what

God dreams of for you instead. We hope you'll catch a glimpse of what it would look like for each of us to love each other and God himself in generosity, faithfulness, thankfulness, contentment, gentleness, humility, usefulness.

Of course God has many more 'new, marvellous, intoxicating' goods in store for you than even that list. But it's a start.

– Andrew Cameron (for the team)

ENDNOTES
1. *Gravity and Grace*, tr. Arthur Wills, University of Nebraska Press: 1997, 120.
2. http://www.whitestonejournal.com/seven.
3. http://www.deadlysins.com.

STILL DEADLY

LUTHER ON GREED
BRIAN ROSNER

To most people greed is hardly a sin, let alone a deadly one. Economists recommend it, politicians rely on it and celebrities flaunt it. 'Who wants to be a millionaire?' is a rhetorical question—the vast majority of people wish they had lots more money. The philosopher's question, 'who am I?' is now best answered: 'I am a consumer—I spend, therefore I am.' In this climate labelling greed a serious sin seems doomed to failure. As psychologist Dorothy Rowe put it: 'Deploring money and its effects is a treasured occupation for those people who like to feel virtuous. ... Doing it is as useful as deploring the fact that we need air to breathe. ... I think that the only way to give up being greedy is to die.'[1] After all, isn't it just a mark of being human to want to have more?

On the other hand, while the tide can hardly be said to be turning, in recent years a number of academics and social commentators have questioned the rampant materialism of the Western world. Put simply, if we want to be rich in order to be happy, it isn't working. Elizabeth Farrelly contends that 'we presume a causal link from desire to happiness, [where] gratified desire equals pleasure and pleasure equals happiness'. The problem with these assumptions is the irony that 'Western happiness has declined precisely in tandem with the rise of affluence'.[2] Sociologists claim that across Western societies self-reported happiness has steadily diminished since the Second World War. As we become habituated to particular pleasures the same pleasures yield less and less satisfaction. This so-called 'satisfaction treadmill' sounds the death knell to contentment and therefore happiness. Ross Gittins claims there is actually 'evidence that those who strive most for wealth tend to live with lower well-being'.[3]

How did we end up in this mess? Clive Hamilton's book, *Affluenza*, compares materialism to a disease. The Western world is in the grip of a consumption binge that is unique in human history. We aspire to the lifestyles of the rich and famous, but at great personal cost in terms of damage to our relationships. We are, he claims, addicted to over-consumption.

This helpful diagnosis is one that Christians have made for centuries in relation to the dangers of greed. In the Middle Ages theologians regarded greed not only as a deadly sin but also as a deadly disease. Greed was commonly thought to be the spiritual equivalent of dropsy, a disease that provoked an insatiable thirst for water even though the body was already filled with fluid. The more the sick person tried to satisfy the thirst, the more it was stimulated until finally death ensued. The comparison with greed is apt.

The Bible actually offers an even more radical condemnation, comparing greed to a religion. Both Jesus and Paul make the comparison:

- Jesus: 'You cannot serve two masters ... You can serve God or money' (Matthew 6:24, Luke 16:13).
- Paul: 'greed is idolatry' (Colossians 3:5) and 'the greedy person is an idolater' (Ephesians 5:5).

Oddly enough, a number of secular thinkers have made the same connection. Two newspapers recently used religious language in their headlines to stories about materialism: 'In greed we trust' (instead of 'In God we trust'); and 'A city obsessed—through its worship of land and buildings, Sydney has found the stories that tell us who we are and what matters in life.' Another example is an obituary for high-profile stockbroker Rene Rivkin, which spoke of his 'once-loyal entourage of supporters who worshipped their high priest at the altar of wealth'.[4]

When it comes to Christian reflection on greed, no one in the history of the church placed more importance on the judgment that 'greed is idolatry' and made more use of it in their preaching, bible exposition and theology than Martin Luther.[5]

BIOGRAPHY OF MARTIN LUTHER

Martin Luther (1483–1546) was a German monk, theologian and dissident whose impact on the world can be felt up to the present day. His translation of the Bible standardised the German language and provided impetus for Bible translation into the everyday languages of people across Europe, including the King James Version in English. His hymns, such as 'A Mighty Fortress is our God', popularised congregational singing. His marriage to Katharina von Bora reintroduced married clergy into the church. Most importantly, his rediscovery of the gospel of justification by faith alone, the doctrine that God declares believers righteous solely on the basis of Christ's death for our sins, sparked the Protestant Reformation.

Luther's opposition to greed ran deep. In 1517 he wrote his famous Ninety-Five Theses objecting to the sale of indulgences by church officials, the practice of soliciting funds with the promise of the forgiveness of sins: 'As soon as the coin in the coffer rings, the soul from purgatory springs.' Luther's pamphlet was nailed to the door of the Wittenberg Church, but, with the aid of the printing press, it was published throughout Germany in two weeks and across Europe in less than two months. Later on Luther nicknamed the Pope who supported indulgences, Avarice of Rome!

Martin Luther on greed as idolatry

Luther's understanding of greed as idolatry may be found at many different points throughout his commentaries and sermons, and even in his catechetical writings and letters. His view is based in part on his interpretation of the Ten Commandments and the close relationship he perceived to exist between greed and unbelief.

In what sense does greed constitute a religion? Luther believed that the sin of greed consisted in *placing confidence and trust in possessions rather than in the living God*. In this way money is the greedy person's god and he or she is therefore guilty of idolatry.[6] Luther's comments on Ephesians 5:5, where Paul brands the greedy person an idolater, explain his understanding of the words 'greed is idolatry'. Speaking of the greedy miser Luther explains: 'since his confidence and loyalty is based on money and not on the living God, who has promised him sufficient nourishment, only money is his god and he may well be called an idolater.'[7]

The first commandment

The foundation for Luther's understanding of greed as idolatry is laid in his treatment of the first commandment, 'You shall have no other gods before me.' Luther does not limit the definition of worship and its counterpoint idolatry to religious adoration and devotion, but takes it broadly to include the idea of trust. In the *Shorter Catechism* he explains how to have no other gods before the Lord: we are to fear, love and trust God above all things. The extensive exposition of the first commandment in the *Larger Catechism*, however, expands on the verb to trust. He defines what it means to have a god in a way that fits both true and false worship:

> A 'god' means that from which you expect to receive all good things and to which you flee in times of need. 'To have a god' means nothing other than to believe and trust from the heart in something. In this sense, as I have already said, trust and faith of the heart define both God and an idol.[8]

According to Luther, to obey the first commandment is to cling to, rely upon and look only to God for whatever one needs in any circumstance.

In order to make clear what it means to trust God he offers some examples that illustrate what it means not to trust God. His first point concerns the rich person who relies upon his or her wealth rather than God: 'Those who set their whole heart on money and possessions in confidence and trust represent the most common form of idolatry on earth.'[9] According to Luther, people set up as their god, that from which they expect and hope to obtain help and comfort. Luther observes that even for pagan religion, to have a god means to trust and depend upon something or someone.

In conclusion Luther contends that we learn from the first commandment a stern lesson about God's claim to our exclusive trust and confidence:

> Therefore, let us learn well the first commandment: God tolerates no rivals when it comes to our trust and demands,

above all, that we put our confidence in him, from whom alone we can expect to receive all good things.[10]

The concluding section of the *Larger Catechism* on the subject of the Ten Commandments stresses the central role of the first commandment, from which all the others proceed. Using a range of metaphors Luther insists that the first commandment casts its bright light over all the others, is the critical stem running through the varied wreath, and is the source and fountain from which all the others spring. To fulfil the first is to obey all ten, including honouring our parents, not committing murder, not stealing, not coveting, and so on.[11] When we obey the other commandments, it should be done by virtue of the first commandment, out of reverence for God. This idea of the interdependence of the Ten Commandments is the basis upon which Luther can understand greed to be a breaking of the first commandment.

Sin as lack of trust in God

Sin for Luther is always an act of contempt for God. He sees it as significant that Moses mentions riches and luxurious living first of all when he explains what causes someone to break the first commandment. Luther interprets this as Mammon and greed: 'When the LORD your God brings you into the land he swore to your fathers ... a land with large, flourishing cities you did not build, houses filled with all kinds of good things you did not provide, wells you did not dig, and vineyards and olive groves you did not plant—then when you eat and are satisfied, be careful that you do not forget the LORD' (Deuteronomy 6:10–13). According to Luther, trusting in riches prevents the human heart from being ruled by faith and love, and consequently the Lord is forgotten. For Luther, Moses understood the first commandment in a spiritual sense, as trust in God, and idolatry as a trust in things.[12]

God as sustainer and provider is crucial to Luther's understanding of the first commandment. Klaus Bockmuehl's study of Luther's confessional writings confirms that according to Luther's catechisms idolatry occurs when human beings over-value earthly, created goods and put their trust in them instead of in God from whom we can expect to have all our needs supplied.[13] Bockmuehl asks, what conception of God lies behind Luther's interpretation of the first commandment? In answer he quotes Luther's *Larger Catechism*, which also underscores the notions of confidence and trust: 'It is essentially God the creator, upon which Luther's explanation draws, or more accurately, God the sustainer, on whom we depend for our body, life, food, drink, nourishment, health, protection, peace and for all our pressing and eternal needs'.[14]

For Luther, whereas belief is trust in God's help, unbelief is trust in oneself and one's own powers, which was often equated with greed. Unbelief and greed grow together; the greater the greed, the more unbelief. When we enjoy material things, without regard for God's will, our soul becomes more and more unhappy. Sin and material prosperity are matched by loss of trust in God and confident hope. The origin of greed is mistrust since stingy people are prone to worry instead of trusting God for their future. Unbelief consists then in having more faith in our own deeds and resources than in God's undertaking to preserve mankind and creation.

Warnings against idolatrous greed

Luther takes seriously the teaching that greed is idolatry not as a piece of intriguing speculation. As a consequence he has much to say about fighting against greed in the human heart by faith.[15] The judgment that 'greed is idolatry' accords the vice of greed great weight, which requires both vigilance and urgency in dealing with it. In terms reminiscent of his famous work against Erasmus, *The Bondage of the Will*, Luther warns believers against a false sense of confidence in their ability to do good, and counsels that they pray for grace in order to be freed from this evil. Rieth explains: 'Luther thought that believers must petition God to learn how to mortify the sin of greed so that their whole being might be rid of it and a new will exist in its place.'[16] In his 1518 exposition of the Ten Commandments he stressed both the depth of human depravity and the effectiveness of contrition and prayer in the fight against greed. Luther took the fourth request of the Lord's prayer, 'give us our daily bread', as a call to shun greed.[17]

In his commentary on Psalm 127 Luther understood verse one, 'unless the Lord builds the house, its builders labour in vain', as a warning against 'greed, anxiety and unbelief' in the family and in society. And in his commentary on the Sermon on the Mount he insists in connection with Matthew 6:31 (So do not worry, saying, "What shall we eat?" or "What shall we drink?" or "What shall we wear?") that a greedy person's worry and faith cannot co-exist: 'Since greed and anxiety are opposed, one must be rid of one or the other.'

Christians who engage in business should, according to Luther, carry out their dealings in faith, that is, in the light of the recognition of God's blessing. If pride in human achievement becomes the focus then greed and worry take over. In a lecture on Genesis Luther commented that Abraham is a model of the relationship between faith and the wrong use of possessions. Abraham does not consistently confess that his goods come from God and this results in robbery and illicit gain.[18]

Not only does greed cause unbelief, the reverse is also true. In an exposition of Psalm 127 Luther stressed his desire that the gospel would produce the fruit of understanding and good works and warned his hearers that the fruit of unbelief, greed, is fighting against this goal.[19] Similarly in his commentary on Matthew 6:25–30 'Do not worry about your life ...' Luther stressed the role of the lily, which by its example refutes human unbelief. Unbelief urges people to 'worry and greed'.[20]

THE APOSTLES' CREED

I believe in God, the Father Almighty, maker of heaven and earth:

And in Jesus Christ, his only Son our Lord, who was conceived by the Holy Spirit, born of the virgin Mary, suffered under Pontius Pilate, was crucified, dead and buried: He descended into hell; the third day he rose again from the dead; he ascended into heaven, and is seated at the right hand of God the Father almighty; from there he shall come to judge the living and the dead.

I believe in the Holy Spirit; the holy catholic church; the communion of saints; the forgiveness of sins; the resurrection of the body; and the life everlasting.

Amen

THE ACQUISITORS' CREED[21]

I believe in Gold, Treasure Almighty, basis of fortune on earth:

And in Greedy Might, the only force that works, which was conceived by primeval folk, born of emergent need, refined in aggressive climate, was modified, strengthened, polished: and defended like hell; and a Third Way arose in its tread; it fermented like leaven, and spreadeth throughout the land, that all should come to judge a bloke by his bread.

I believe in owning shares; the lowly plastic crutch; the extension of credit; the retention of gain; the reclamation of debt; and in life without fasting.

Amen

Trust, confidence and idolatrous greed

Luther's understanding of greed as idolatry in terms of a contest between God and money for our trust has a firm basis in the Bible. Trust and confidence are defining characteristics of the greedy with respect to their wealth, idolaters in relation to their idols and of believers in connection with God. Numerous texts not only observe that the rich trust in their riches, but warn that such reliance is incompatible with and an unacceptable alternative to trust in God.

The Prophets and wisdom writings warn that wealth can be an object of trust. In Jeremiah 48:7 the prophet accuses Israel of trusting in her 'strongholds and treasures'. Psalm 52:7 states that the one who 'does not make God his refuge ... trusts in his great wealth' (cf. 49:13,15). Proverbs notes, 'the wealth of the rich is their fortress' (10:15) and 'their strong city' (18:11); but 'those who trust in their riches will wither' (11:28).

In contrast to the rich who are tempted to trust in their riches, God is the only trust of the poor and those of humble means (Psalm 34:6; 40:17; cf. 68:10; 86:1; Isaiah 66:2). Proverbs 18:10–11 suggestively juxtaposes trust in God and trust in money: 'The name of the Lord is a strong tower, where the righteous may run for refuge. A rich man's wealth is his strong city, a towering wall, so he supposes'. In Proverbs 28:25 'a greedy person' is contrasted with 'the one who trusts in the Lord'.

Trust and confidence is also a frequent description of what people do with their idols. In the Song of Moses in Deuteronomy 32:37–38 the Lord asks about the idolatrous Israelites: 'Now where are their gods, the rock they took refuge in ... let them rise up to help you! Let them give you shelter.' So too in Isaiah 44:9 the idol worshippers say to their idols, 'save me, you are my god'. According to Habakkuk 2:18 the one who fashions an idol 'trusts in what he has made'.

On the other hand, the Songs of Trust in the Psalter (4, 16, 23, 27, 40, 46, 62, 115, 125, 129) express eloquently the believer's and the believing community's dependence upon God. Not only is the verb 'to trust' frequently used in these prayers, but also a host of synonymous expressions which expound its meaning. Such trust is said to belong exclusively to the Lord; the Lord *alone* gives safety (4:8); he *only* is the believer's salvation (62:1) and rock (62:2). Similarly, in Psalm 81:8–10 the motivation for not having a foreign god is the Lord's promise to supply life's needs: 'Open wide your mouth and I will fill it' (81:10b; cf. v. 16).

Significantly, two of the alternatives to trusting God in these Psalms are idols and riches. In Psalm 115:2–8 lifeless 'idols of silver and gold' are contrasted with 'our God [who] is in heaven'. Verses 8–9 make plain the choice between trusting either idols or God:

> Their makers grow to be like them,
> and so do all who trust in them.
> But Israel trusts in the LORD;
> he is their helper and their shield.

Likewise Psalm 40:4 affirms: 'Blessed is the man who makes the Lord his trust, and does not turn aside to false gods.' Furthermore, God's people are exhorted to 'trust always in God' and to 'pour out your hearts before him' (Psalm 62:8). Verse 10 warns against trusting in wealth in the same terms: 'Do not trust in extortion, and take no pride in stolen goods: when wealth increases, do not set your heart upon it.'

Such teaching is repeated in the New Testament. In the parable of the rich fool in Luke 12 Jesus labels as 'foolish' what we might call prudent investment as a means of security: 'I will ... build bigger barns and there I will store all my grain and goods.' In 1 Timothy 6:17 the apostle counsels the rich not to trust in their riches but in God. The notion of trusting God not money is also apparent in the instructions to the disciples in the mission charges (Mark 6:8–9 for example), in the story of the widow's offering (Mark 12:41–44), the calling of Peter and Matthew to leave all and follow Jesus (Mark 1:18–20; Luke 5:28), the example of Zacchaeus (Luke 19:1–10), the call to store up treasures in heaven not on earth (Matthew 6:19–21) and supremely in Matthew 6:25–34, where the disciples are advised to take notice of God's provision for the birds and the lilies. Hebrews 13:5–6 encourages its readers not to love money with the promise of the Lord's help, implying that faith in God is the alternative to finding security in money.

Surviving the deadly sin of greed

When it comes to understanding greed, Martin Luther is 'right on the money'. While no one admits to it, greed is a religion with millions of devoted adherents. From Luther we learn that in the fight against greed we need more than just the help of psychology, sociology and economics—at root greed is a theological problem. The driving motivation of greed is our need to find security and confidence in a dangerous and uncertain world. Money is a god from which we expect to receive all good things. But like any other idol, money is a god that fails to deliver and is not worthy of our trust. The god of money inevitably leads its worshippers to disappointment and humiliation.

Luther's teaching gives us a number of vital tips in dealing with this deadly sin:

1. Recognise the seriousness of the sin of greed—it is a form of idol worship that arouses God's jealousy.

2. Resist the urge to immoderate accumulation of wealth that grows out of a lack of trust in God.

3. Seek contentment and be generous and willing to share—in order to deal with greed that consists of both unrestrained grasping and selfish hoarding.

4. Appreciate the natural world—greed arises when we forget that God is our creator and sustainer. Go bird watching, hiking, gaze at the sunset, grow vegetables, keep chickens.

5. Wait expectantly for the resurrection—we put too much stock on material things when we think that they are all that exists. Keep a loose grip on this world, for this world in its present form is passing away.

6. Aim to get *really* rich—God has many new and marvellous things to engross those who know him and are known by him.

What would Martin Luther say to Donald Trump?

'Money, Money, Money, Money … MONEY!!' A man in an expensive suit with unusual hair alights from his private jet. So runs the opening sequence of the television show 'The Apprentice', now in its sixth season. In it legendary American entrepreneur, casino owner and property developer Donald Trump (born 1946) puts a group of wide-eyed wannabes through their paces in cut-throat New York before offering one of them the opportunity of a lifetime. Ever keen to spread the word, 'the Donald' is the author of such books as *The Art of the Deal*, *The Way to the Top*, *Surviving at the Top*, *The Art of the Comeback*, *Think Like a Billionaire* and *How to Get Rich*. What would Luther say to Trump?

Luther was a strident and sometimes fiery preacher. However, as *Table Talk*, one of his most popular books indicates, he was also someone who enjoyed a long conversation over a meal with a beer in hand and he was used to talking with powerful figures like Trump. He would probably invite Donald for dinner at his home. After getting to know him, he might ask him some searching questions:

'Mr Trump, your personal wealth and lavish lifestyle remind me of a German count, an Austrian aristocrat, a Swiss baron or maybe even a Roman Pontiff. However, you mentioned that things did not always go your way, citing your 1999 bankruptcy, from which you recovered in part with the help of an inheritance from your father, and the 2004 'restructuring' of your casino resorts.

'Did these 'unfortunate' experiences cause you to question whether material wealth is trustworthy, whether it is in fact an illusory and unstable foundation upon which to build your life? Where did you flee in these times of need, to the promises of money that had previously let you down, or to the God who created you and sustains your life? Have you considered whether in your amazing drive to the top you may have substituted money for the living God as your supreme trust?

'Donald, all human beings, whether rich or poor, owe God an insurmountable debt, because of the selfish and greedy ways in which we live. The good news is that God offers to foot the bill through the sacrificial death of his Son for our sins! All he asks is that we offer him the trust only he deserves. What prevents our doing this is often our failure to acknowledge our own bankruptcy. You did it once materially. Is it time to do it spiritually, this time allowing your heavenly Father to bail you out?

'The apostle Paul had some good advice for those like you who are rich in this world (see 1 Timothy 6:17–19). He told them not to be arrogant nor to put their trust in wealth, which is so uncertain, but to put their trust in God, who richly provides us with everything for our enjoyment. I commend your efforts in philanthropy and charitable giving. Indeed, Paul says to do good, to be rich in good deeds, and to be generous and willing to share. Above all, take hold of that which is truly life.'

A Murder of Crows[22]

a murder of crows
a parliament of owls

a weight of albatrosses
an army of ants

a bellowing of bullfinches
a business of ferrets

a charm of finches
a flamboyance of flamingos

a skulk of foxes
a gaggle of geese

a tower of giraffes
a bloat of hippopotamuses

a mischief of mice
a buffoonery of orangutans

an ostentation of peacocks
a squabble of seagulls

an ambush of tigers
a wake of vultures

a sneak of weasels
a deceit of lapwings

a pride of lions
a greed of humans

ENDNOTES

1. Dorothy Rowe, *The Real Meaning of Money* (London: HarperCollins, 1997), ix, 184. Rowe's own view is that greed for something other than money is the way forward, a position not that different from Christianity's recommendation that people seek to become 'really rich', instead of just rich.

2. Elizabeth Farrelly, 'In search of a cure for paradise syndrome', *The Sydney Morning Herald*, 28–29 October 2006, 28.

3. Ross Gittins, 'How to be happy', *The Sydney Morning Herald*, 2 January 2006.

4. Ian Verrender, 'Pity the poor man', *The Sydney Morning Herald*, 3 May 2005, 8.

5. A comprehensive history of interpretation can be found in the author's book, *Greed as Idolatry: The Origin and Meaning of a Pauline Metaphor* (Grand Rapids: Eerdmans, 2007). For a book-length exploration of the significance of idolatrous greed for Christians today, see *Beyond Greed* (Kingsford: Matthias Media, 2004).

6. The most thorough and perceptive treatment of Luther's view of greed is in German: Ricardo Rieth, '*Habsucht' bei Martin Luther* (AKT 1; Weimar, Böhlau, 1996). The relationship between greed and idolatry is covered on 152–58, upon which this exposition summarises and builds.

7. D. Martin Luthers Werke: Kritische Gesamtausgabe (Weimar, 1883ff) 17,11, 211, 4–20.

8. *Werke* 30.I:133.

9. Ibid.

10. *Werke* 30.I:139.

11. Christof Gestrich, *The Return of Splendor in the World: The Christian Doctrine of Sin and Forgiveness* (Trans. by Daniel W. Bloesch; Grand Rapids: Eerdmans, 1997), 181 comments wryly that the logic of Luther's view leads one to conclude, 'the reason they are even there [the instructions of the second table] is that God foresaw man's universal failure to keep the first commandment'.

12. WA 14, 612, 29 – 613, 16; in this connection he also mentions 1 Tim 6:10; Bar 3:17.

13. Bockmuehl, *Gestz und Geist: Eine kritische Würdigung des Erbes protestantische Ethik* (Giessen/Basel: Brunnen, 1987), 57.

14. Ibid.

15. See Rieth, *Habsucht bei Martin Luther*, 158–62.

16. Rieth, *Habsucht bei Martin Luther*, 162.

17. WA 19, 96, 7f. For a contemporary exposition of the first commandment which builds on Luther's interpretation see Traugott Koch, *Zehn Gebote für die Freiheit: Eine Kleine Ethik* (Tübingen: J.C.B. Mohr, 1995), 157–73.

18. *WA* 15, 366, 11–19; 43, 298, 38–299, 5.
19. *WA* 115, 377, 26–378, 4.
20. *WA* 32, 464, 38 – 465, 7.
21. Written by Richard Firmin, for the author's *How to Get Really Rich: A Sharp Look at the Religion of Greed* (Leicester: IVP, 1999), 121.
22. All but one of the lines is drawn from *A Parliament of Owls: A collection of collective nouns* (Penguin, 2005).

AUGUSTINE ON LUST
ANDREW CAMERON

King David had at least six wives and five concubines.[1] Yet still he lusts after Bathsheba and felt compelled to sleep with her. The adventurer and diplomat Giacomo Casanova claims in his memoir to have had sex with 122 women. Various sportsmen, actors and male celebrities are reported from time to time as having slept with dozens or even hundreds of women. Men reading this chapter, who may have slept with only one or zero women, have moments when they wish they were King David, Casanova, or the others.

Let's face it: this is a chapter about men, by a man in conversation with another man, about something particularly experienced by men. The extent to which the reflections of this chapter are of use to women will be for them to judge, but what is perhaps most 'useful' is that it concerns men taking responsibility for their sexual thoughts and feelings. Like the biblical authors, Augustine did not turn male sexual lust into a woman's problem. He opposed those who blamed women, and even now he reminds men that each man finally has to do business with this vice.

However, we may find that Augustine's investigation helps all who struggle with intense sexual thoughts and feelings, whether male or female. And he may assist us in our other desperate longings, whether sexual or not.

Augustine's defence of the body

But—what are we playing at here? Why would sexual thoughts and feelings be something to 'struggle' with? Casanova surely didn't. The infamous womanisers of fiction and history—Don Juan, James Bond, Rasputin, and so on—would laugh at the idea of sexual thoughts and feelings being a 'struggle'. They wouldn't care if we called them 'lustful', and would suggest that lust is only a 'struggle' because we call it a 'struggle'. If you just go with it, the 'problem' goes away and becomes fun.

Therefore many objectors argue that Christians 'struggle' with sexual thoughts and feelings because Christianity has bred a subtle but deep hatred of the body and its sexuality. Some also blame Augustine as the founder of such attitudes. For one commentator, Christianity displays a 'hatred of this world and of the body'.[2] She thinks Augustine helped to shape this view by teaching that our errors of judgment are 'rooted in the body itself and its sexuality'[3] since people's bodies are just 'incidental accretions from the world of sin'.[4]

People who despise the body and demonise sexual desire can be found in all religions and ideologies, not only among Christians; but Augustine was certainly not one of them.

> There is no need, then, in the matter of our sins and vices, to do injustice to our Creator by accusing the nature of flesh, which, of its own kind and in its due place, is good. But it is

not good for anyone to forsake the good Creator and to live according to a created good ...[5]

In other words, our sins and vices are not the fault of our physical 'flesh', which God has made good. That assertion is bedrock for Augustine. 'The nature of the original fault had, for Augustine, nothing essentially to do with the creation of the body'[6] because 'Augustine had come to a firmly-rooted idea of the essential goodness of created things'.[7] He also discovers the excellence of the body through Jesus Christ:

> [T]he good and true Mediator showed that it is sin which is evil, and not the substance or nature of the flesh. He showed that a body of flesh and a human soul could be assumed and retained without sin, and laid aside at death, and changed into something better by resurrection.[8]

Augustine's high view of our sexuality is connected to his high view of the body, for 'what pertains more closely to a body than its sex?'[9]

How good goes bad

What really interests him, though, is the way something so good can often 'malfunction' to produce great evil. Augustine sums up another of his great themes when he observes that 'it is not good for anyone to forsake the good Creator and to live according to a created good'.[10] Evil happens when we lose perspective, when we *stop seeing things as they really are,* when some good thing is no longer enjoyed in its 'due place' but as an end in itself and we desert God for it. This logic of good things 'malfunctioning' brings Augustine to speak against what he calls 'concupiscence'—those *strong desires* that spring from within our bodies, by which we are sometimes propelled into evil. We can be 'concupiscent' for all sorts of things: power, food, money, recognition. We can also be 'concupiscent' for sex, which is what is usually meant by the term 'lust'.

It is worth noting that sexual lust was not a major focus in Augustine's investigation of concupiscence. For example, the first reference to sexual lust in his enormous *City of God* occurs after fourteen and a half chapters, and then only as one among a list of many strong desires that humans typically experience. Conversely, when he specifically addresses sexual lust, he immediately thinks of our other strong desires as well.[11]

Augustine was fascinated by the common denominator between sexual lust and other kinds of strong desire: the way humans seem to be *voracious* and *insatiable* for what is good. We fall into the trap of thinking that because a thing is desirable we can never get enough of it. We switch into a kind of overdrive to soak up as much of the good thing as we can. The desperation that people display from infancy for everything good is seamless with the desperation that many people experience, as adults, for sex.

BIOGRAPHY OF AUGUSTINE

Augustine was born in 354 and died in 430, which made him remarkably long-lived for his time. He grew up on the Roman empire's North African fringe during the final days of its imperial greatness.

Although his mother was a Christian, the young Augustine's middle-class classical education left him unimpressed with Christianity. His lifestyle was littered with belief systems, youthful excess, and careerist obsession. But when 'chance' events coincided with a troubled mind, at thirty-two Augustine converted to Christianity.

He thought he would become a Christian philosopher.

But a visit to church in an African regional town near his birthplace resulted in him becoming their priest in 391, and not long after, their bishop. Augustine pastored, preached and wrote in this role until his death. His early years were opposed to the body-hating 'Manichees'; his middle years dealt with the century-old church-split involving rebel 'Donatists'; and his final years restrained the stern moralism of the self-assured 'Pelagians'.

His life straddled the 9/11 of his day—the first sack of Rome in 410. Rome was supposedly the 'eternal city', but its security had been breached in the first of many death-throes. Augustine used these events to point to the truly eternal City of God, pleading with Romans to become members of this city of real peace rather than bloody Roman 'peace'

Augustine was good at describing what people needed in Jesus. Even today, his Scripture-based, experience-grounded insights continue to bring freedom and to show how Jesus can be said to bring true life.

Augustine's revolution (and his mistake)

When he does turn to examine sexual desire specifically, Augustine tries to imagine what sex would be like between Adam and Eve before they committed the first human sin. This is obviously a key moment in what Augustine thought about sex. If he really thought that human sexual desire is a sin springing from a faulty body, then he would imagine that Adam and Eve started out as non-sexual beings. Of course the Bible says no such thing. Genesis describes nakedness and a joining to become 'one' in verses that are overtly sexual (2:24–25), and which share the

Bible's generally joyous and erotic optimism about married sex. But subsequent to biblical times, some sub-Christian thought implied that the 'sin' committed by Adam and Eve was their having sex. Is this Augustine's view?

When he imagines them having sex in a sin-free time and place, his vision of this sexual intercourse is a vision of deep peace.[12] He makes one mistake, to which we will return in a moment. But he pictures sex for this innocent couple as being a thankful, joyful, bodily, pleasurable and honest love. So much is the body and sexual pleasure *not* regarded by Augustine as sinful or offensive, that scholars have found he offered a revolutionary *antidote* to the views of his contemporaries. Paul Ramsey shows how Augustine's deep affirmation of human sexuality is actually his *distinguishing* feature.[13] According to Peter Brown, who is an expert in ancient attitudes to sexuality and the body and also Augustine's foremost biographer, 'the pace of his thought on sexuality was set by firm if courteous disagreement with other Christians and upholders of radical ascetic ideals,' against whom Augustine gives 'a call to moderation'.[14]

> He had come to envision, in a manner far more consequential than many of his Christian contemporaries, Adam and Eve as fully sexual beings, capable of ... a glorious intercourse, unriven by conflicting desires, without the shadow of sin upon it. ... two fully physical bodies follow[ing] the stirrings of their souls, 'all in a wondrous pitch of perfect peace'.[15]

So where does Augustine go wrong? He imagines that Adam would have been able to give his semen to Eve without the involuntary moment of orgasm. This view seems very strange, and it is; but in order to discover what drove it, we need to pause and remember the way Augustine was puzzled by human concupiscence in general.

He is trying to unravel the mystery of human desperation for what is good. What could cause us to act in such demented ways about good things? Babies crave desperately for good things in a way that blends into the way adults crave for good things. Perhaps the father's orgasmic moment of intense desire, which inaugurates human conception, is to blame. Perhaps this moment of a father's 'lust' commences the continuum of human voracity that appears in all people even from infancy. Augustine's view of 'original sin' then follows: human concupiscence, both sexual and otherwise, is a judgment from God in response to Adam's strong desire to eat the fruit, to 'know good and evil', and to be 'like God'. Ever since, humans are conceived in a concupiscible moment, live concupiscible lives from infancy to death, and so are in solidarity with Adam. (These ideas are used in a discussion with Augustine's Pelagian opponents, which is beyond our scope.) Augustine concludes that sexual lust is a just punishment for humanity—a loss of rational control for a race who had so brazenly sought to seize control.[16] On this view, the problem with concupiscence is the way it overthrows our 'reason', or *our ability to see how things really are*. The involuntary nature of our sexual arousal is, he thinks, a miniature example of this overthrow.

But Augustine has overstated his case. Eight centuries after Augustine, Thomas Aquinas observes that to stop thinking too hard during sexual intercourse and just enjoy it, does not mean we have overthrown the order of reason![17] That is, we do not stop seeing things as they really are just because we sometimes put thinking on hold for a bit. After all, we do the same when we fall asleep.

In fact Augustine knows that his account has some problems when it comes to marriage. He thinks sex finds its proper home in *marriage*, and so he becomes a bit tangled when trying to defend marriage while also defending his account of sexual lust. Augustine thinks that although a residue of sexual lust remains within marital intercourse, '[c]arnal concupiscence ... must not be ascribed to marriage: it is only to be tolerated in marriage. It is not a good which comes out of the essence of marriage, but an evil which is the accident of original sin.'[18] Sexual pleasure in marriage can be 'honourable'.[19] The 'carnal delight' of marriage 'cannot be lust', he says, when 'used' rightly.[20] 'in the indispensable duties of the marriage state,' sexual concupiscence 'exhibits the docility of the slave.'[21] But his defence of married sex is a bit strained, if only because a desire is not really 'concupiscent' when it is 'docile'! More to the point, a man whose project is to honour his wife until death does not engage in sexual desire in the same way as a womaniser, who lives for his desire and *not* for the woman. The first man lives for his wife in precisely the kind of loving devotion that God wants from married men. Of course 'docile' is not the best word for this kind of sexual desire: wives generally do not want 'docile' husbands! But this picture of sexual desire that is 'docile' as a 'slave' tries to distinguish between sexual lust that serves only itself, and sexual desire that serves a wife and builds a marriage.

So Augustine is a bit fanciful to equate the involuntary nature of sexual desire and orgasm with the overthrow of reason; and he gets a little tangled when trying to defend the good of married sex. But even if his account needs revision at these points, it does perhaps highlight some truths that we easily forget. Modern Westerners love to imagine that *we* have arrived, that ancient views like Augustine's have nothing to offer, and that modern Western sex is all about freedom, liberation and fun. But by wrestling with whether concupiscence even threatens marriage, Augustine reminds us that sexual desire and its expression are not always untrammelled delight. There are darkly terrible secrets stalking our state of modern sexual 'enlightenment', ranging from disorders of desire that damage and deaden marriages, through to sexual obsessions that require imprisonment. These would come as no surprise to Augustine. He knows that even married people walk in the same wilderness into which Adam and Eve were cast. Married sex is no longer always a 'glorious intercourse' where two bodies follow the stirrings of their souls in a wondrous pitch of perfect peace, uncut by conflicting desires. We do well to keep listening to Augustine on lust.

Lust's real problem (from bitter experience)

Augustine's account is on stronger ground when he asserts a fundamental difference between sex within a marriage as compared to sex outside of a marriage. This kind of sex exemplifies people living for their desires, rather than their desires serving someone. For what would propel people to have sex without the commitment of marriage? In these arrangements, sexual concupiscence 'plays the king',[22] or as we might say, is in the driver's seat. He sorrows over the breakdowns in relationship that follow from this use of sex. Men become isolated, women are devastatingly disappointed, and children are scorned.

Augustine did not come to this conclusion on theoretical grounds, but from bitter personal experience. He tells of the sadness and ambiguity he caused when he took a young concubine. The story is unbearably poignant. 'I lived with a woman ... a mistress whom I had chosen for no special reason but that my restless passions had alighted on her.' Here, again, was lust 'playing the king'. As is often the case with sexual activity, a loving companionship of sorts did grow: 'she was the only one and I was faithful to her.' Yet this was 'a bargain struck for lust, in which the birth of children is begrudged' ('though, if they come', as a son did in his case, 'we cannot help but love them.') It turns out that when a 'real' wife was chosen for Augustine, his mistress 'was torn from my side as an obstacle to my marriage', 'which crushed my heart to bleeding, because I loved her dearly.'[23]

We glimpse in this story all the hallmarks of what modern people still find when they live for sexual desire rather than enjoying it in service of something greater. Although sex obviously is designed for children, unmarried sex despises children. Although the 'bargain' struck between sexual couples is not for permanence, the role of sex to generate and nurture lifelong companionship is realised too late when lovers are torn from each other's side. Men like to imagine that women are recreational objects, but sex creates powerful bonds of affection that are painful to break. Augustine's lust was not for her good; she probably wept in anguish once used and rejected.

Yet his folly is not yet complete. While on the way to his 'real' marriage, he is impatient for sex and in consolation he takes another mistress, 'more [as] a slave of lust than a true lover of marriage'. He doesn't say too much at this point, but suggests that the marriage itself is thus marred, in part because 'the wound that I had received when my first mistress was wrenched away showed no signs of healing.'[24] Sexual lust has turned the goods of sex and marriage into something melancholy and scarred, deranging and distorting relationships that held so much promise and could have been so good.

What can be done for poor, stupid, concupiscent humans? The point of marriage is to create a space of peaceful order where all the goods of sexual relationship can be enjoyed. Marriage is a shelter where peace begins to be found. In 'the restraint of the marriage alliance, contracted for the purpose of having children',[25] children can be a welcome fruit of sexual desire. Men learn how to calm and heal their disordered desires, ceasing to range over all humankind, so that one person becomes the grateful and constant focus of their desire. Married people's sexual arousal is glorious, when it is directed toward the marriage partner and toward the conception of children.[26]

Augustine's advice

We began with some womanisers who evidently did not think of sexual lust as a struggle, but abandoned themselves to it. What would Augustine say to them? In a sense, nothing. He knew their world.

His *Confessions* (where we read about his concubine) make strangely melancholic reading. Its background 'canvas' is alive with earthy blessings: fertile ground, good food, a vibrant natural environment. Layered upon this canvas are a network of social goods: a loving family, good schooling, the bustle of a city, friends, and spouses. All the little human figures in the story move about on a massive, richly woven tapestry of riches, benefits, excellences and goods.

Against this backdrop of plenty, we read of various conquests in concupiscence: for professional advancement, for friends, for inclusion and recognition, for food, for knowledge, and (we could almost forget!) for sex. It is as if Augustine and his friends are drowning in a sea of plenty; but by grabbing desperately at titbits, life is experienced as a never-ending problem of scarcity. Augustine only ever sees abundance as scarcity, and responds in concupiscence. He has lost the capacity to see things as they really are.

Yet throughout the book he says 'accept my confessions, O Lord,'[27] and we come to realise that Augustine's 'confessions' are apologies—rueful admissions that God's presence and generosity were always in plain view, but Augustine had lost the capacity to see.

Augustine knows the world of the womaniser. He knows what it is to be so obsessed by lust that no other way makes sense. The capacity for such human blindness is a marvel to Augustine. His reflections on it echo those of Paul the apostle, made four centuries previously, that 'the outlook of disordered human nature is opposed to God, since it does not submit to God's Law, and indeed it cannot' (Romans 8:7, NJB).

However if Augustine were to have a go at persuading the womaniser, he would clarify that the problem of concupiscence is *not* that it points to whatever is pleasurable; and the problem of sexual lust is *not* that it leads to sex. The real problem is the way it deranges relationships. The womaniser who does not care for the women he uses is known by those around him, especially the women, as a problem to be avoided rather than a cause to be celebrated. But what of womanisers who claim to 'love' women? For them, love is just another kind of hunger. Augustine would ask them—what if love is *not* always hungry, but just content? What if not all love is from hunger? What if love sometimes simply recognises a woman as precious, and treats her accordingly? What Augustine did to his mistress shows that lustful love is finally chaotic and cruel. But contented love can honour one woman for life. Only this kind of love gives a basis for justice and a common life together.[28]

In the event that some slave to lust wants out, Augustine knows that there are answers to be had, both for someone who wants to change after a lifetime of lust, and for anyone who knows Christ but still struggles with lust.

Flee to the Mediator. Augustine's whole life and work is an amazed response to that 'good and true Mediator' who 'showed that a body of flesh and a human soul could be assumed and retained without sin … and changed into something better by resurrection.'[29] But Jesus Christ is a 'mediator' at this point, not an 'example'. That is, we do not know and follow Christ in order to imitate our way to goodness. If that were possible, then 'Christ died for nothing' (Galatians 2:21). Augustine's fight with the Pelagians pivots upon this verse: if the solution to lust were within our grasp, then Christ died for nothing. But God is not that stupid. Christ's death for sin implies our desperate and hopeless need for one who will 'mediate' between us and God. With Christ as mediator, God forgives our ongoing concupiscent failures, and then gives us his Spirit who begins a deep change in us.

Stop singling out *sexual* lust. Of course we have done precisely that in this book, by calling it a 'deadly sin'! But Augustine wasn't interested in this medieval way of dividing up sins. He thought that sexual lust was one of many lusts that plague us. Augustine was far more disturbed by our lust to dominate one another, as seen in the Roman lust for power. Indeed, it has been argued that later Augustine's thinking about sexual lust was singled out for display because the post-Constantian empire needed to downplay his attacks on the lust for power, and did so by emphasising his writings on sexual morality.[30]

Sexual lust, then, is often only one aspect of an overall profile of concupiscence. Do you live to eat, or shop, or travel? Are you envious, or controlling, or desperate to belong, or hungry for recognition? If we think that people and things are generally ours to consume, then of course we will think the same about sex. It will also seem to us that there is *never enough* for us to consume: we will act as if good things are scarce, and we will desperately try to suck them up wherever we see them. We won't deal successfully with lust until we take on this overall lifestyle of desperate voracity.

Settle it, don't stoke it. With the exception of married sex, sexual desire seems to work by 'positive feedback'. Stoking it only makes it worse. If we drink salt-water at sea to ease our thirst, there is a moment of relief, but then a more raging thirst. Likewise with lust: a cycle of positive feedback makes it addictive, like alcohol or heroin. One internet porn user says 'after a not very long break, I start missing porn. I need to get that hit again. And I feel like there's nothing else in life to look forward to.'[31] (Breaking these cycles of addiction may need the support of communal fellowship and a trained professional.)

Augustine saw this cycle when he observed that although lust generally decreased for the elderly, occasionally it increases in an old person who abandons himself to it. But the cycle of sexual desire also works in the other direction. It can be settled and calmed. Augustine notices the way it decreases for the 'sexually continent',[32] by which he means those in whom sex and sexual desire has found its proper home. As we have seen, one proper home is marriage. Married men who are struggling with lust may need to begin or restart a painful but rewarding process with their wives: apologising for neglect, asking for changes, rediscovering what his wife would like, and suggesting new ways forward. (A reputable trained counsellor may help this process.)

The other proper home for sexual desire, and Augustine's personal practice, is chaste singleness. Paradoxical as it may sound, chaste singleness that remains open to the possibility of marriage is a serious proposal for handling lust. When single people engage in a prosperous network of friendly relationships of service, it is the *absence* of any sexual favouritism in this network that holds them steady.

The ongoing barrage of sexual stimulation we endure is a new development. Perhaps dealing with this barrage should be thought of as part of a wider project, to take control of *all* messages we hear that instruct us to consume. Perhaps we can rediscover how truly boring the television, news media and magazines really are. Perhaps by removing those things from our lives for a time, we might find pleasure again in playing with kids, in coffee with friends, in long walks with our spouse. Perhaps we could rediscover that vast tapestry of plenty within which we are already situated, but which we do not see when we are so busy trying to suck up the tasty titbits that modern media wants to sell us.

Try thankfulness. The *Confessions* are also a picture of an ongoing life of thanks, breathing out glory to God for all the good that is there. Augustine's practice is obviously based upon the biblical authors' myriad practices of thanks and praise. There is not space to list them here; but in biblical logic, thankfulness is the antidote and vaccine for concupiscence. Once we have begun to breath out thanks for all that we have, we begin to see properly again. Little by little, greed becomes boring and pointless.

Remember the future. One of the strangest aspects of Christian thought is the way reflection upon the future often brings calm to the present. Augustine longs with Paul for 'redemption of the body' (Romans 7:24) in the kingdom of heaven, 'where there shall be not only no guilt for sin, but no concupiscence to excite it'.[33] Having to wait is a bit sad. But it is also a relief. For it brings great hope to know that the struggles of the present are not the last word. They are passing, and the little changes that the Holy Spirit makes for people now, are a glimpse of and a down-payment towards this brilliant new future.

ENDNOTES

1. David's wives include Michal (1 Samuel 18:27), who is withdrawn by her father Saul (1 Samuel 25:40) but taken back by David (2 Samuel 3:14f); Ahinoam and Abigail (1 Samuel 27:3, 2 Samuel 3:2-3); Eglah (2 Samuel 3:5); additional unnamed wives (2 Samuel 5:13); and eventually Bathsheba (2 Samuel 11:27). Three other women, Maacah, Haggith and Abital, may be concubines (2 Samuel 3:3-4) and additional concubines are unnamed (2 Samuel 5:13).

2. Martha C. Nussbaum, 'Augustine and Dante on the Ascent of Love', in *The Augustinian Tradition*, ed. Gareth B. Matthews, (Berkeley; London: University of California Press, 1999), 86 n.13.

3. Martha C. Nussbaum, 'Morality and Emotions' in *Routledge Encyclopedia of Philosophy*, ed. Edward Craig, 10 vols., vol. 6 (London: Routledge, 1998), 561.

4. Nussbaum, 'Augustine and Dante', 81.
5. Augustine, *The City of God Against the Pagans* tr. R.W. Dyson, *Cambridge Texts in the History of Political Thought* edition, (Cambridge: Cambridge University Press, 1998), 588 (XIV.5).
6. Margaret R. Miles, *Augustine on the Body* vol. 31 (Missoula: Scholars Press, 1979), 67.
7. Peter Brown, *Augustine of Hippo: A Biography* (London: Faber, 1967), 325.
8. Augustine, *City of God*, 426 (X.24).
9. Ibid., 195 (V.7). Augustine directed this comment against ancient misogynists, in defence of the good of womanhood.
10. Ibid., 588 (XIV.5).
11. Cf. Augustine, *On Marriage and Concupiscence* ed. Philip Schaff, tr. Peter Holmes and Robert E. Wallis, NPNF 1, vol. V (Grand Rapids: Eerdmans, 1987; originally published New York, 1887), 272 (I.20), where sexual lust is just a species of the more generic 'lusts' of 1 John 2:15–17.
12. Augustine, *City of God*, 629 (XIV.26).
13. Cf. Ibid., 628-30 (XIV.26) for his account of sexual intercourse in paradise; and cf. Paul Ramsey, 'Human Sexuality in the History of Redemption', *Journal of Religious Ethics* 16 no. 1 (1988), 62 & passim.
14. Peter Brown, *Augustine of Hippo: A Biography (A New Edition with an Epilogue)* (London: Faber, 2000), 500.
15. Ibid., 501, citing a letter by Augustine discovered comparatively recently (Divjak 6*). On this basis, Brown hotly disputes the 'egregious cultural narcissism' that blames Augustine for Western sexual discontents [502], even branding one recent treatment 'a travesty' [518 n.69].
16. Augustine, *The City of God* ed. Philip Schaff, tr. Marcus Dods, *NPNF 1*, including On Christian Doctrine, vol. II (Grand Rapids: Eerdmans, 1988; originally published New York, 1886), 614-18 (XIV.16–18); Augustine, *Marriage and Concupiscence*, 266 (I.7).
17. Thomas Aquinas, *Summa Theologica* tr. Fathers of the English Dominican Province, (London: Benzinger Brothers, 1937), vol. 19, 83–84 (3a.supp.41.3.ad6).
18. Augustine, *Marriage and Concupiscence*, 271 (I.19).
19. Ibid., 291 (II.22).
20. Augustine, *On the Good of Marriage* ed. Philip Schaff, tr. C.L. Cornish, *NPNF 1*, vol. III (Grand Rapids: Eerdmans, 1988; originally published New York, 1887), 407 (§18).
21. Augustine, *Marriage and Concupiscence*, 269 (I.13).
22. Ibid. (I.13).
23. Augustine, *Confessions* tr. R.S. Pine-Coffin, *Penguin Classics* edition,

(Harmondsworth: Penguin, 1961), 72 (IV.2).

24. Ibid., 131 (VI.15).
25. Ibid., 72 (IV.2).
26. Augustine, *Marriage and Concupiscence*, 274 (I.25). Augustine speaks of 'illicit' uses of sex within marriage, by which he probably means sexual activities that cannot result in conception. While discussion of this matter should be pursued elsewhere, a quick summary of Christian discussion about contraception is needed here. Roman Catholic moral thought has tended to judge married sexual play, with Augustine, on a 'per-act' basis. If a given sexual act cannot result in children, it is deemed wrong. But Protestant moral thought concluded that the goods arising from marriage—sexual pleasure, companionship and children—are appropriated 'per-marriage'. Therefore Protestants tolerate contraception and enjoy many forms of sexual play in the context of a *marriage* that is gratefully open, over time and fertility permitting, to the bearing and sustenance of children.
27. E.g. Augustine, *Conf.*, 91 (V.1).
28. Augustine, *City of God*, XIX.21.
29. Ibid., 426 (X.24).
30. Gerald I. Bonner, 'Libido and Concupiscentia in St Augustine', in *Studia Patristica: papers presented to the Third International Conference on Patristic Studies (Oxford 1959)*, ed. Frank Leslie Cross, vol. VI (Berlin: Akademie-Verlag, 1962), 312–14.
31. Cited in Simon Castles, 'In the grip of a guilty pleasure', *The Age*, 8 October 2006; online: http://www.theage.com.au/news/in-depth/gripped-by-a-guilty-pleasure/2006/10/07/1159641569552.html (accessed 21/12/2006).
32. Augustine, *Marriage and Concupiscence*, 275 (I.28).
33. Ibid., 279 (I.38).

STILL DEADLY

BASIL OF CAESAREA ON ENVY
BILL SALIER

One of the few explicit statements of motive concerning the death of Christ, names envy: 'It was out of envy that they handed him over...' (Mark 15.10). This is one of a series of references in Scripture. In the Old Testament a number of Proverbs warn against envy (Proverbs 3:31; 14:30; 23:17; 24.1). In the New Testament, envy is seen as a typical sin of those who have rejected God (Romans 1:29; Galatians 5:21; Titus 3:3) and therefore is not appropriate for followers of the Lord Jesus (1 Peter 2:1).[1] Alongside these references are a host of stories and incidents illustrating the destructive effects of envy and implicitly warning readers about its presence and influence (Cain and Abel, Saul and David, the two women disputing about a child before Solomon).

Envy has long been a regular on lists of the seven deadly sins. It is described as a capital or cardinal sin because from it flow all manner of other sins such as rivalry, enmity, hatred and violence.

In lists of the sins it often occurs second to pride though one rather suspects that it would like to be first! Envy is often seen as the flipside to pride. At the essence of both is the notion of comparison. If after comparing yourself with another you feel superior, then pride results; if you feel inferior then it is envy.

Reflection on envy is not confined to biblical writers and Christian thinkers. It was Petula Clark who sang 'the other man's grass is always greener' before concluding with an appeal to 'just be thankful for what you've got'. Her song is at one with a long and ancient line of reflections on envy. Aristotle's description of envy as 'a kind of pain at the sight of (another's) good fortune' is echoed by Cicero, Plutarch and a host of other thinkers down to Aquinas and beyond. Aquinas also described envy as a kind of sadness with a selfish or malevolent bent to it. More recently Freud famously spoke of penis envy and its place in the formation of feminine sexuality and identity.

While envy has generally been seen as an undesirable trait, the sociologist Schoeck is among a few who defend a certain form of envy as important in the development and maintenance of the modern world.[2] If we didn't envy, he suggests, there would be no incentive to further ourselves and develop new ways of living and being. (His observation is not entirely new however, as it reflects the thought of the Old Testament writer in Ecclesiastes 4:4.) Nevertheless the positive voices are few and far between with envy generally recognised as a destructive vice with no redeeming features.

It is arguably the most difficult sin to recognise and admit. There is a sense of shame attached to its presence and even an admission of inferiority if one confesses to envying another. Its effects are directed at the destruction of the neighbour. Consequently it is denied, re-named or simply ignored and left to run rampant.

BIOGRAPHY OF **BASIL OF CAESAREA**

Basil the Great is best known for his work as one of the Cappodocian fathers in the great Trinitarian debates of the fourth century AD. Along with Gregory of Nyssa and Gregory of Nazianzus he was instrumental in combating the Arian heresy, that denied the divinity of Christ. Born (c. AD 333) one of ten children at Caesarea Mazaca in Cappodocia (modern day eastern Turkey), Basil was educated in the finest pagan and Christian culture of his day at both Constantinople and Athens. He became a monk and then led a hermit's life until called to be the Bishop of Caesarea in Palestine, following the death of Eusebius in AD 370, in order to combat the Arians. He is known as an eloquent, learned, statesmanlike and pugnacious person with a great concern for personal holiness. He also had a talent for organisation and was important in the shape and ethos of eastern monasticism. He has left a legacy of theological, pastoral and ethical writings as well as collections of homilies.

Some distinctions

Jealousy is a close cousin of envy; the so-called 'green-eyed monster'. Often jealousy, covetousness and hatred are confused or conflated with envy. They are not the same, although they are often used interchangeably.

The difference is that we are jealous of what we already have and envious of what other people have. Jealousy guards while envy seeks to steal or destroy. Jealousy may be a defensive or even admirable posture. Occasionally we speak about jealously protecting a relationship or something that is, by some sort of right, our own. Envy is destructive and other-person directed in its effects. It wishes active harm on another. If jealousy is the green-eyed monster then perhaps we might want to describe envy as a squinty, malevolent, grey-eyed monster.

In both the Old and New Testament Scriptures the same Hebrew and Greek words, respectively, can be translated as both jealousy and envy. When referring to God, however, these words used are never translated 'envy' but rather 'jealousy'. The Bible happily describes God as a jealous God, jealous to protect the relationship he established with his people. He is never described as envious. After all what does he not possess that another does? And what is there in another that he could want? He wishes only good for his neighbours. He is jealous for the relationship that he has with his people and expresses indignation at threats to that relationship.

Covetousness and greed are second cousins of envy. Covetousness and greed are aimed at the good things that another has while envy targets the person. Envy is often content with not possessing the desired good so long as the other person loses or is diminished in their enjoyment of that good. Greed and covetousness hoard, and perhaps plot to steal, while envy seeks to destroy the other.

With some of these distinctions in mind let's take a closer look at envy with the help of Basil of Caesarea. Basil of Caesarea is best known for his theological reflection with respect to the great christological controversies of the early church but he was also a pastor and a preacher. One surviving homily concerns the topic of envy.[3] Basil has not been chosen for his particular insights so much as the way in which he encapsulates much of the ancient perspective on envy: its nature, its dangers and its 'cure'. We might well term his contribution an anatomy of envy. Basil's thought also anticipates much that remains true of envy in our own time, so we will have opportunity to move between

Basil's thought and some contemporary expressions of the points he makes as well as note some further developments.

Basil on envy

Basil defines envy as 'pain caused by our neighbour's prosperity'. In saying this he is echoing the classical definition formulated by Aristotle. Basil points to the unlimited potential for envy because our neighbours will prosper in many different areas: fertile fields, prosperity, handsome looks, mental capacity, reputation in the community and so on. There is much to envy apart from the other man's grass.

Basil suggests that envy is spiritually, socially and personally dangerous.

Envy is a spiritual problem. From a spiritual perspective envy is related to the devil. Here Basil echoes ancient Jewish teaching as expressed in Wisdom 2:24, 'but through the devil's envy death entered the world, and those who belong to his party experience it'. It is clearly not of God and this leads to the major exhortation of the sermon: shun envy. If the Devil is condemned for envy how much more so the one who walks in his envious footsteps. Envy is a sure sign of the impending judgment of God and is therefore not to characterise those who claim to follow God (cf. Galatians 5:21; 1 Timothy 6:4; Titus 3:3; 1 Peter 2:1).

Envy is a social problem. From a social perspective Basil makes a number of observations. He observes that envy is evil because it actively wishes our neighbour harm and rejoices in the evil that befalls him. We are instead to wish our neighbour good and to actively seek his or her good. Love does not envy (1 Corinthians 13:4).[4] Basil points out that the envious man not only grieves over his neighbour's good fortune but also looks for his downfall and then weeps with him. While weeping with the neighbour might look like empathy, Basil suggests that it is tainted. It does not arise from sympathy but merely the desire that the misfortune may appear in a worse light. We catch a glimpse of this when in sympathising we enumerate our neighbour's woes, reminding her of the great fall she has suffered, deliberately compounding the suffering.

Envy can also take action against the neighbour by damning with faint praise and turning virtue into vice. The envious person calls the courageous man reckless, the temperate woman callous, the just man severe and the clever woman cunning. In doing so the enjoyment is sapped from life as no virtue is recognised; the good in life is not appreciated and attention is fixed upon rottenness.

At the most extreme end of the social aspect, people will often take action against an envied neighbour through gossip, slander and even more overt forms of physical harm.

Basil emphasises the fact that we do not envy strangers but rather neighbours, close relatives and friends. He puts it this way, 'Envy is the plague of friendship'. This is wickedly echoed by Gore Vidal who observes, 'Whenever a friend succeeds, a little something in me dies'. This observation rings true to life.

Basil also points out that people knew that it was not good to be envied. They did not want to fall victim to the envious (or evil) eye, believing that a gaze could cause harm. This was a well-known and feared phenomenon in the ancient world and a variety of talismans, magic spells, and other elaborate devices were devised to ward off its effects. Basil resists the more superstitious elements of this belief but does not dismiss its reality, attributing the effects of the evil eye to the Devil.

Basil's observations have their reflex in our contemporary situation. First, while not necessarily believing in the evil eye, there is still a (diminishing?) sense that it is not good to be envied and that it is best to keep one's success to oneself. With respect to the closeness of envy it is observed that we rarely envy too far up the pole—it is those around us who are the problem. It might be one's peers from high school, met at a reunion some 20 years after leaving, where the comparison between houses, cars and spouses kills. Research into this phenomenon found that many people would rather make $50 000 per annum in a neighbourhood with an average income of $40 000 per annum than $100 000 in a neighbourhood with an average of $150 000.[5] Like envies like. The arts, science and music worlds are replete with stories of rivalry and envy. The businessman does not envy the sculptor in the same way as he envies another businessman. Alain de Botton makes a similar point in his recent book. In a discussion of increasing affluence and democracy, he notes that the more people 'we take to be our equals ... the more people there will be to envy'.[6]

Finally, while we might not actively seek our neighbour's harm, we can feel a sense of delight when harm befalls him or her. Envy's presence is revealed through the frisson of *schadenfreude*, the malicious joy that bubbles up at the fall of a great one or even one that is only slightly greater then you. Who has not felt some delight at hearing about burglar alarms being set off in rich homes, Mercedes being towed away or the owner of a Porsche receiving a ticket for some kind of misdemeanour?

Arguably this is expressed at a national level in Australia via the so-called 'tall poppy syndrome'. This is evident in the variety of magazines that grace supermarket checkouts. In these the reputations of the rich and famous are shredded on the covers of Famous, New Woman and the National Enquirer for sins such as too much cellulite, not enough body mass or being caught in one of many possible compromising positions or simply being the victim of a poor photo that presents the celebrity in an unflattering light. Why do we think that somehow they deserve it? While there may be some kind of social benefit in the deconstruction of celebrity, we probably ought to recognise a large dose of simple envy in our delight at these front pages. Of course this is not confined to distant celebrities. As the French essayist La Rochefoucauld observes, 'We always find something that is not displeasing to us in the misfortunes of our best friends'.

Envy is a personal problem. Basil notes that envy's effects are often personal, internal to the envier. There is a sense of shame attached to envy and its antipathy towards the neighbour; even a sense of inferiority. Envy is the sin that dare not speak its name for it is an admission of inferiority as well as bringing further honour to the envied. The only remedy for the envious man is to rejoice in his neighbour's fall into misfortune. This too must be kept to oneself, for it is shameful to delight in grieving over the good fortune of another. And by keeping it 'inside' envy does its damage. Basil expounds at some length on the harmful effects of envy, asking who ever diminished his neighbour's good by feelings of annoyance.

The effects of envy upon the envier are manifold. Basil uses the language of being consumed and pining away from grief. The envious can be recognised by their faces—their eyes are dry and lustreless, their cheeks sunken, their brow contracted. Their mind is distorted and confused by passion and they are incapable of making valid judgments in handling affairs. In all this Basil continues a long tradition describing these physical effects of envy. Statues of envy personified depict people strangling their own throats or being choked by snakes. Other visual representations suggest an emaciated figure, wasting away through envy or desire of the other.[7]

Envy is a fatal disease according to Basil. It places us in a hostile relationship to God, our neighbour and our own selves. It ruins our life, perverts our nature, and arouses hatred of the good bestowed on us by God. It leads to hypocrisy and double-dealing in relationships and eventually kills relationships. Envy is the sickest of sins, sated only by the destruction of the object of desire.

The cause of envy

Basil doesn't particularly deal with the cause of envy; he is more interested in the fact of it. However it is worth a moment to pause and reflect on some attempts to explain the roots of envy. There is some social-scientific research conducted with respect to the ancient Mediterranean world that tries to account for the presence of envy. This research suggests that the ancient world is best characterised as an honour/shame society where issues of honour and status were of vital importance.[8] At the same time it was a society in which there was a concept of limited good. This means that all goods are limited in quantity and are already fully distributed. That is to say there is only so much gold, land, praise, honour and fame to go around. The upshot of this was that if someone seemed to be gaining in one or another of these goods then it must be at the expense of someone else who would be decreasing in these goods. Statements reflecting this understanding can be found in Plutarch, Philo and Josephus. The quote in correspondence from Fronto to Marcus Aurelius illustrates the point and connects it with envy: 'set yourself to uproot and stamp out one vice of mutual envy and jealousy amongst your friends, that they may not, when you have shown attention or done a favour to another, think that this is so much taken from or lost to themselves. Envy among men is a deadly evil and more fatal than any, a curse to enviers and envied alike'.[9]

Others have suggested that the source of envy is insecurity. The envier is often one who can appreciate the envied's talent with absolute clarity. The film *Amadeus* captured this in its examination of the composer Salieri's envy of Mozart. In the film, Salieri recognises the brilliance of Mozart and acknowledges his superiority, only to fall prey to envy and eventually seek to destroy him. Perhaps the ancient world's conception of limited good is not so ancient. Envy kicks in when we perceive that our chances for happiness are threatened by another's flowing locks, flashy car, or outrageous talent. When we stand to miss out on life's prizes, on what we think we deserve or could achieve, envy's brand of hostility and inferiority surges through us.[10] And does this insecurity reflect a more basic insecurity that derives from tacit acknowledgment that before a holy God we are not the people we are meant to be? When we meet another person who is superior in some small or large way, who has what we appear to lack, we are reminded that in some more profound way we do not 'measure up'. We project this on to our neighbour in some form of envy.

The French literary theorist Rene Girard provides a further perspective here as he contemplates envy. His thought has exerted a considerable and growing influence in Christian circles, especially in respect to thinking concerning the nature of the atonement and the relationship between God (and therefore Christians) and violence.[11]

We are particularly interested in one aspect of his thought that relates to envy: his notion of mimetic desire. Girard states that desire is properly basic to what it means to be human but that it doesn't arise from the individual's exercise of autonomy or even as the function of a relationship between the individual and a particular object of desire. Rather our desire is mediated by others. We desire things because others desire them. I want what you want, he suggests, not because the thing desired is necessarily or intrinsically attractive or because I am a free agent exercising desire where I like, but rather because you desire it. I copy your desires and then our desires feed off each other. My desire for the particular object or quality further fuels your desire for the object or quality. Eventually this leads to a situation of rivalry.

In Girard's full-blown theory this notion of mimetic rivalry then leads potentially to violence between us as we fight for the desired object. The only way out of this cycle of desire and potential violence is for either one of us to 'win' or for a scapegoat to be found; a third party against whom we can both turn and victimise. Peace returns as we fight the common enemy together.

The classic illustration given is one that is familiar to parents all over the world. Two children are playing side by side when one finds a particular toy. Her playmate, as soon as she sees the other child play with the toy desires that toy. She envies her neighbour. The desires are inflamed and potential violence ensues until either a parent intervenes or a scapegoat comes along. The scapegoat is a third child. The first two children find a reason to gang up on the third child and their differences are resolved as they unite against the scapegoat.

Girard is firstly a literary critic and he suggests that the great and lasting literature is that which acknowledges and analyses this 'playground' mechanism at work. A fascinating analysis of Shakespeare called *A Theatre of Envy* demonstrates Shakespeare's discovery and development of envy and mimetic rivalry throughout his plays.[12] Girard argues that Shakespeare's work abides because it exposes what we all intuitively perceive and partake in, though we dare not or, perhaps, cannot admit it.

In time Girard develops this insight into a full-blown anthropology and says that this mechanism accounts for the growth of society and religion. Our interest is not so much in the development of the whole of the theory but rather in the truth embedded in the analysis of envy or mimetic desire/rivalry. Girard shows how ingrained this sort of thinking is to who we are as people. It is 'there' almost all of the time and it is not related to things but rather to people. This is a profound analysis of something akin to original sin, with envy as its root, though he does not describe it this way.

Dealing with envy

We have strayed some distance from Basil and it is time to return. We have examined his anatomy of desire and noted the reflex and extension of some of the ideas he discusses in the contemporary setting. All in all, his is a penetrating and sobering analysis.

Basil moves on from this analysis to suggest a remedy, as all good pastors must. He suggests two. First, that the goods of this world ought not be regarded as either great or admirable. Believers are to fix their eyes not on the transitory but rather on possessions that are real and eternal. The rich are not to be envied for their money, or position but it is what they do with these things that counts: they are to be pitied if they use them for evil or their own good (for they will be judged) and to be lauded if they use these goods for the service of God and neighbour.

Second Basil suggests that if we desire glory, then we are to pursue it through virtue. This is within our command in a way that wealth, physical vigour, and beauty are not. In this Basil is a child of his times. He urges his congregation to flee envy not through desire of ascent to God but rather through the love of honour. His congregation knew that there was nothing more valuable in life than gaining and preserving honour, acting with a love of honour and being acknowledged as doing so.

But we must ask if Basil's solution is deep and theological enough. Has he recognised the depth or magnitude of the problem? Much modern advice concerning envy makes a similar underestimation.

One of the simplest solutions to the problem of envy is 'to arrange to acquire everything you want in life'. This is of course a counsel of despair, and in all likelihood would not deal with the problem anyway. Similarly suggestions such as: 'find your niche, move to a poorer neighbourhood where you will compare better; flourish in a puddle; don't compete where it doesn't matter to you; curb comparisons; remind yourself that high status does not equal high happiness' offer helpful advice but in most cases do not deal with the root of the problem.[13]

Another alternative is to rehabilitate envy along the lines of Schoeck's analysis mentioned above. Envy, it is suggested, has a positive role in building civilisations. Without envy we wouldn't aspire and try to improve ourselves. Envy is the foe of drab levelling it is suggested, it arouses a passion for discrimination, degree and difference, all the things that make life interesting. All this appears to underestimate the destructive force of envy and forget its 'outgoing' nature, against others, as suggested by Basil.

Perhaps there is a 'good' sense of envy that encourages productive dreams and aspirations, but this may be better referred to as admiration or emulation.

Girard's 'solution' advances an aspect of Basil's thought and points to a better way when he rightly states that desire is not in and of itself the problem; it is the object of desire that is the issue and he suggests that instead of envying others we emulate or imitate the person of Jesus who shows us the 'mimetic-desire-free' life.[14]

However, if envy is a sin, and as deeply ingrained as Girard's broader analysis suggests, then the 'solution' must lie in more than our ability to transfer misplaced desires. It must be dealt with by the grace of God, operative through the forgiveness won by the Lord Jesus at the cross. This offer is responded to by confession and repentance. It is only in this broader context that emulation of the Lord Jesus' model of other person centred love that drives away envy can take place. In this context the perception that we live in a society of limited good, where the exaltation of another suggests to us that we are somehow missing out can be proven to be false as Jesus reveals to us a wise, generous creator and Father who has infinite resources at his command. In Jesus we can find the love and acceptance that answers the problem of the 'plenty' that we see in others and as lacking in ourselves. We find that we are loved while sinners and are caught up in a plan for our renewal that makes us heirs of all things and renewed in the image of our creator.

A personal note

This has been a challenging topic to explore personally. The extent to which I have discovered I am 'primed for pettiness' has been shocking. This is best observed in my response to the 'slings and arrows of outrageous fortune' experienced by colleagues and friends. I am challenged afresh by the example of John the Baptist as recorded in John's Gospel. John's disciples were concerned that all John's followers were leaving to follow Jesus. Such 'success' was provoking envy. John's reply reflected the words of one who was totally secure in his knowledge of God and his place in the Father's plan: 'He must increase; I must decrease' ... (John 3:30). This is based on John knowing that he has not achieved anything on his own—it has all been given him from above; from knowing his own role with respect to Jesus and being content with that; and finally seeing his relationship to Jesus as friend and not rival; he therefore rejoices in his friend's success. There is no need, indeed there is no place, for odious and envy provoking comparisons in the Kingdom of the Christ.

What would Basil say to the Gucci Company?

The Gucci Company is one of a number of companies that markets products under the brand name *Envy*. Other companies include a limousine hiring service and a brand of clothing. In Gucci's case it is a range of perfumes and eau de toilettes for men and women. What would Basil say?

I suspect that he would express first his shock at such a casual usage of such a dangerous idea. And then to think that it is being used to sell a product apparently on the premise that its use would make others envious of you! He would point to the dangers of envy both socially and personally, not the least the idea of the evil eye of those who envy another. I suspect Basil would question the wisdom, if not the morality, of a company who would encourage such a thing.

As he got to know our modern culture he might perceive that this is merely a marketing tool, that perhaps it is meant ironically and that he ought not to take it so seriously. To this he might respond that he notes, along with the other so-called deadly sins, that envy has been trivialised by this kind of thing; perhaps even glorified. And that this process can only lead to further harm as people fail to recognise envy or remain subject to its temptations unchecked and continue to reap the spiritual, social, and personal consequences he has so vigorously outlined.

His suggestion to pursue honour will seem a little quaint in the modern age and one wonders how a perfume called *Honour* would sell. Nevertheless Basil would stick to his guns and point to the need to expose envy for the spiritual, social, and personal danger that it is and the necessity to flee from it, not glorify it by labelling a cheap scent (well an expensive scent, but a scent nonetheless).

Finally he would ask those who are being encouraged to trivialise the place of envy in their lives by this kind of labelling to consider their attitudes and behaviour; to flee envy and pursue an appropriate goal for their legitimate desires and search for regard. Doubtless he would do this in a stern and unyielding fashion!

ENDNOTES

1. The Greek word used in the NT references is *phthonos* and cognates. It is usually translated envy. This word is not found in the Greek translation of the OT canonical books though it does appear in a couple of Apocryphal

books. There are also a cluster of references using the Greek word *zelos* and cognates that can be translated as either envy or jealousy. These words are used in the Greek translations of the Proverbs verses cited above. The context will determine whether *zelos* is translated jealousy, zealous or envy. Occasionally a translation will use jealousy when perhaps envy would be better and vice versa, indicating the fine line that exists in sense between jealousy and envy.

2. H. Schoeck, *Envy. A Theory of Social Behaviour.* Indianapolis: Liberty Fund, 1969[ET].

3. All discussion about Basil's work on envy is based on Saint Basil, 'Homily 11: Concerning Envy'. Trans. St. M. Monica Wagner, C.S.C. in *Saint Basil. Ascetical Works.* The Fathers of the Church. A New Translation. Vol 9. Washington: The Catholic University Of America Press, 1962, 463–474.

4. Here is a case where the Greek word, *zelos*, which can be translated envy or jealousy is usually translated as envy because love can, properly, be jealous. Christian love seeks good and not evil for its enemies and so cannot envy in the sense described (cf Matthew 5:43–48).

5. R.H. Frank, *Choosing the Right Pond. Human Behavior and the Quest for Status.* New York: Oxford University Press.

6. A. de Botton, *Status Anxiety.* London: Penguin, 2004.

7. A selection of ancient representations of envy can be found in *Jahrbuch für Antike und Christentum* 26 (1983), Tafeln 1–8.

8. A.C. Hagedorn & J.H. Neyrey. '"It was out of envy that they handed Jesus over" (Mark 15:10): The Anatomy of Envy and the Gospel of Mark', *JSNT* 69 (1998), 15–56.

9. 'Fronto to Marcus Aurelius as Caesar'. C.R. Haines (trans). *The Correspondence of Marcus Cornelius Fronto.* LCL. Cambridge, Mass: Harvard University Press, 1982, Vol I, 73.

10. De Botton speaks of the importance of the amount of love and regard we are accorded with respect to our self-confidence. *Status Anxiety*, 16.

11. An overview of Girard's work including key excerpts can be found in J.G. Williams (ed.) *The Girard Reader.* New York: The Crossroad Publishing Company, 1996.

12. R. Girard, *A Theatre of Envy.* Oxford: University Press, 1991.

13. These suggestions are among those listed by C. Flora, 'How to get over status anxiety', *Psychology Today* 38.5, 2005, 46–50.

14. See 'The Goodness of Mimetic Desire', 62–65 of *The Girard Reader.*

CLEMENT ON GLUTTONY
RICHARD GIBSON

Food is the new sex, according to the late night advertisement that punctuated the coverage of the cricket from England a few years ago.[1] What sounded like a sassy piece of social observation was, in fact, a teaser for an upcoming show about three chefs and their restaurants.[2] Just a case of dressing up glutton as glam, in an attempt to boost ratings? Or are we in the midst of a culinary revolution that will do for food what the sexual revolution did for sex over the last half century? Just think, with the eroticisation of the humble meal, we can look forward to a new era of food-abuse, people eating but never being satisfied, families shattered by addictions, and more lonely men, eating alone in front of flickering computers. An era when gluttony will come into its own.

Eating as a moral issue

The origin of the claim, 'food is the new sex,' has been traced to an anonymous magazine headline from 2001.[3] Since then, serious social analysts have taken it up as a commentary on contemporary Western culture. As Jerome Barkow, a social anthropology professor at Dalhousie University in Halifax, explains:

> 'Mass media has done something that once I would have said was flat out impossible. They've actually managed to make sex boring. So, what do you do now to get the juices flowing, to get excited, to get angry?' asked the soft-spoken professor who researches and teaches about evolution and human nature. Increasingly the answer involves food choices and body image.

Intriguingly, in a culture that increasingly refuses to disapprove of people's sexual preferences and behaviour, diet and body-shape has become a moral issue. Barkow observes: 'Food is a class marker because being overweight shows that you are immoral, you're overindulging, you lack willpower, you lack self-control.'[4]

Gluttony: the deadliest and most sinful?

It could be that our culture already regards, at least implicitly, gluttony as the most sinful and deadliest of the traditional seven. The old-fashioned, medieval-sounding label, 'gluttony', is rarely used, but the confluence of health and morality issues surrounding over-eating have taken it to the top of the ratings. The scientifically informed headline 'Fat can be fatal. Obesity is the great new global health scare'[5] has become the staple diet of current affairs programs, with sensationalised stories about fat children being taken from their neglectful parents. Industries grow up around the yo-yoing weight of chat-show hosts. Reality programs with chillingly ironic titles, like *Biggest Loser,* thrive. In our culture, there are few bigger losers than the obese, those who lack the will-power to change. There is unprecedented documentation and widespread recognition that in prosperous Western cultures, we are eating ourselves to death.

Ordinarily, this would be too good an opportunity for Christian commentators to pass up. Rarely do traditional categories of sin and such widely recognised social epidemics pass so closely to each other in their orbits. Today, Paul's cry: 'Wretched man that I am. Who will rescue me from this body of death?' (Romans 7:24),[6] is more likely to resonate powerfully with the average person's struggle to lose weight, than any struggle to overcome covetousness or lust. Here, surely, is the opportunity to dust off traditional discussions of gluttony, to draw on ancient Greek and Christian discussions of self-control (*enkrateia*) and the powerlessness to change (*akrateia*), in order to offer a searching critique of a sin, a sin finally being recognised as deadly and sinful.

This would represent a revolution for 'gluttony'; a significant tarting up of what is, traditionally, the dowdiest and least convincing of the moral failures. In the most oft-quoted assessment, Dorothy Sayers says, 'Gluttony tends to be, on the whole, a warm-hearted and companionable sin, often resulting from, and in, a mistaken notion of good fellowship.'[7] Some of the traditional accounts seem to admit the failure of gluttony to possess the 'bite' of other sins. They tend to broaden the discussion of gluttony to incorporate any kind of indulgence or excess. There is clearly value in this more diffuse treatment. However, it seems to reflect embarrassment at finding gluttony in the same company as some of the 'spiritual' sins, such as pride, envy, or lust, which receive the most trenchant and theological critiques in the pages of Scripture.

Reasons to abstain from 'obesity-bashing'

There continue to be a number of biblical and practical reasons that should discourage Christian commentators from rushing too eagerly to join the rising contemporary chorus against overeating and obesity. Most of the biblical reasons revolve around Jesus. In one of the rare uses of the word in the English Bible, Jesus cites an accusation levelled against his ministry: '...the Son of Man came eating and drinking, and they say, "Look, a glutton (*phagos*) and a drunkard, a friend of tax collectors and sinners!" Yet wisdom is vindicated by her deeds' (Matthew 11:19; cf. Luke 7:31–35).

Undoubtedly, there is some exaggeration in this charge, to present Jesus in the worst light; to portray Jesus as the 'stubborn and rebellious son' condemned in Deuteronomy 21:18–21 to death by stoning. But there was something about the way Jesus mixed with people and enjoyed their hospitality, to which the Gospels, especially Luke's, bear consistent testimony (Luke 5:29). The contrast with an austere ascetic like John was striking, and drew comment.

Second, Jesus himself was unambiguous that food did not render anyone morally unclean: 'He said to them, "Then do you also fail to understand? Do you not see that whatever goes into a person from outside cannot defile, since it enters, not the heart but the stomach, and goes out into the sewer?" (Thus he declared all foods clean.)' (Mark 7:17–23). This text can hardly be cited to prove that the consumption of food never becomes a moral issue, but it does counsel caution in demonising food in general, and certain foods in particular.

Third, by his incarnation and teaching, Jesus affirmed the goodness of the created order. Throughout church history Christians have been lured to stringent austerity, imposing regulations like, 'Do not handle, Do not taste, Do not touch'. In Colossians 2:21–23 Paul warns that regulations have the 'appearance of wisdom in promoting self-imposed piety, humility, and severe treatment of the body, but they are of no value in checking self-indulgence'.

Similarly, 1 Timothy 4 warns that the demand for abstinence from certain foods made by some teachers ultimately derives from 'deceitful spirits and teachings of demons'. Their error lies in the fact they forbid food, 'which God created to be received with thanksgiving by those who believe and know the truth'.

Finally, Jesus, in keeping with the Old Testament, sees the banquet or feast as an appropriate image for the nature of the kingdom of God and the end-time. There is something about this picture, with its elements of gracious host, abundant provision, deep satisfaction, and fellowship around a common table that carries the associations Jesus wants to convey. Several parables (Matthew 22:2–9; Luke 14:15–24; 25:10) echo Isaiah's great hope:

> On this mountain the LORD of hosts will make for all peoples
> a feast of rich food, a feast of well-aged wines, of rich food filled
> with marrow, of well-aged wines strained clear (Isaiah 25:6).

To his closest friends, in the context of a meal, Jesus offered this great promise:

> You are those who have stood by me in my trials; and I confer on
> you, just as my Father has conferred on me, a kingdom, so that
> you may eat and drink at my table in my kingdom, and you will
> sit on thrones judging the twelve tribes of Israel (Luke 22:28–30).

To these biblical considerations can be added some practical concerns. Too often in the past, attacks on the glutton have glibly assumed that the corollary of gluttony is excessive weight. In this sense, the glutton has been the most visible of the seven deadly sinners. Sadly, Christian speakers and writers, who should be more aware of the consequences of the fallen world for such neat correlation, have fallen into this trap. To his credit,

Anthony Campolo records his shame after preaching against gluttony:

> Of the sermons I wish I had never preached, none elicits more regret than a sermon on gluttony ... The cruelty was not apparent to me at the time. When I preached the sermon, I was convinced that the obesity of those in the congregation was due to a lack of willpower on their part and a decision to let themselves go physically ... I had no understanding of the complex factors contributing to a problem which afflicts so many.[8]

Campolo goes on to outline some of these complex factors, including inherited and chromosomal disorders, chemical balances, and psychological disorders. There is nothing Christian about clubbing soft targets with blunt instruments, however well-intentioned.[9]

Conversely, Christians must guard against conspiring with one of the false gods of our age, and inflicting harm on another group at the other end of the scales. In one of the most thoughtful and perceptive treatments of the topic, Mary Louise Bingle exposes the prevalence and dangers of America's national obsession with thinness:

> To fit into the bastions of privilege (or at least to elude the assaults of prejudice), we must fit into smaller and smaller clothing sizes, in defiance of the ethnic morphology of our bodies—and even in defiance of their natural maturation. The cult of slenderness which amplifies class and race differences links to a cult of youthfulness as well ... In our patriarchal culture, such harshness indisputably targets women more fiercely than men.[10]

Unsurprisingly, women are massively over represented in another modern epidemic: eating disorders such as anorexia and bulimia. Tragically, Christian preachers and authors often reinforce these ideals and unwittingly feed these terrible disorders with titles like *Pray Your Weight Away, More of Jesus Less of Me, Help Lord—the Devil Wants Me Fat!* and *Thin, Trim, and Triumphant.*[11] No-one can afford to write on the dangers of gluttony without taking into account the horrors of anorexia and bulimia, lest careless comments add to the difficulty of dealing with them. If it seems to be irresponsible not to target overeating in a culture that is eating itself to death, it needs to be remembered that many are also dieting themselves to death.[12]

BIOGRAPHY OF CLEMENT OF ALEXANDRIA

The surviving biographical information about Clement is decidedly thin. As best we can tell he was born around AD 150, probably in Athens, and arrived in Alexandria, North Africa, about AD 180 as a recently converted Christian. His writings reflect an intelligent and wide-ranging thinker, well educated in pagan literature and philosophy. In that great city he attached himself to the Christian teacher Pantaenus. Around 200 he took over the privately operated 'school' and could number the great Origen amongst his pupils.

Scholarly assessments of Clement vary widely. He is regarded as the father of systematic, Christian theology, but whether this is a compliment depends on how this hybrid of biblical revelation and Greek philosophy is evaluated. More than a century ago, Swete waxed eloquent: 'Perhaps nothing in the whole range of early patristic literature is more stimulating to the modern reader than his [Clement's] great trilogy of graduated instruction in the Christian life.'[14] On the other hand, Jülicher thought that only his unintelligibility as a writer kept him from being rejected as a heretic by the early church. [15] *In turning to him for advice about food we need to be wary of Clement's attraction to the Greek dualism of body and soul, and to the Stoic ideal of self-sufficiency.*

Ancient wisdom on food abuse

But for anyone who knows a bit about him, Clement of Alexandria may seem a curious choice as a pilot through the troubled waters between the skillet of indulgence and the carob-disc of asceticism. As someone writing at the turn of the third century AD, Clement would seem unqualified to offer guidance on such modern problems. More importantly, he is known for being affected by Greek philosophy's negative view of the physical world. In a famous passage, of his most significant work, he insists that Jesus didn't really need food, but ate so that the disciples would not become suspicious of his alien physiology. This sounds a lot like the ancient heresy of Docetism, which claimed that Jesus only seemed to be human, which reflects a Greek concern to distance Jesus from real bodily existence. [13]

Clement provides one of the most sustained, thoughtful, and powerful analyses of food use and abuse in extant Christian writings. In doing so, he draws on the Scriptures, an array of ancient sources, and his own experience and observation of dining in one of the great cosmopolitan cities of any age. A number of his comments warn against dismissing his perspective as ancient and obsolete. At one point, he bemoans, 'the unbalanced and unhealthy and miserable state of men such as athletes fed on an enforced diet'. The cult of the gymnasium and minimal body fat was alive and well in his day, along with the self-starvation it feeds.

Clement avoids simply putting the boot into the visibly overweight. His discussion remains focussed on the behaviours he wishes to criticise. The chapter on gluttony in *Christ the Educator*[16] is framed by references to Philippians 3:19: 'Their end is destruction; their god is the belly (*koilia*); and their glory is in their shame; their minds are set on earthly things.' For Clement, the chapter is directed at people 'who trust in their belly', rather than trusting God. Construing Philippians in this way may reflect Clement's ascetic tendency rather than Paul's intention, but it would be a misunderstanding shared with many commentators.

Abuse 1: Excessive preoccupation with food. Clement's analysis of food-abuse in ancient Alexandria falls into two parts. The first critiques the craving for new and more exotic taste sensations, rendered by most translations as 'gourmandising'. It is regrettable that such an archaic term persists for such a thoroughly contemporary phenomenon, but it is hard to find a satisfactory verbal form. This Clement defines as 'nothing more than immoderate use of delicacies'. Such people are not satisfied by a plain, simple diet. The availability of fresh produce creates the necessity of constantly filling their mouths with something more delicate and rare:

> I feel pity for their disease; but they themselves show no shame in flaunting their extravagances, going to no end of trouble to procure lampreys from the Sicilian straits and eels from Maeander, kids from from Melos and mullets from Sciathis, Pelordian mussles and Abydean oysters, to say nothing of sprats from Lipara and Mantinean turnips and beets from Ascra. They anxiously search for Methymnian scallops, Attic turgots, laurel thrushes, and the golden brown figs for five thousand of which the notorious Persian sent to Greece. On top of all this, they buy fowl from Phasis, francolins from Egypt and peacocks from Medea. Gourmands that they are, they

greedily yearn for these fowl and dress them up with sweet sauces, ravenously providing themselves with whatever the land and the depth of the sea and the vast expanse of the sky produce as food. Such grasping and excitable people seem to scour the world blunderingly for their costly pleasures, and make themselves heard for their 'sizzling frying-pans,' wasting the whole of their lives in hovering over mortar and pestle, omnivorous fellows who cling as close to matter as fire does.

The self-indulgence of such people extends beyond the main course, and they receive their just desserts for their lack of restraint. 'Truly, in ever inventing a multitude of new sweets and ever seeking recipes of every description,' laments Clement, 'they are shipwrecked on pastries and honey cakes and desserts'.

There are a number of strands to Clement's prosecution of such behaviour. Some of them are practical. Excessive variety of food leads to some nasty consequences such as physical illness, indigestion, and 'perversion of taste'. Many have learnt the lesson for themselves very painfully, after 'some misguided culinary adventure or foolish experiment in pastry cooking'. Clement claims it is a 'natural law' that those who follow a simple diet 'are stronger and healthier and more alert'.

He can also cite biblical texts in support. Proverbs 23:3 warns, 'Do not desire the ruler's delicacies, for they are deceptive food.' Clement takes the words of 1 Corinthians 6:13 'Food is meant for the stomach and the stomach for food, and God will destroy both one and the other' to be an explicit curse on gluttonous desire. At other points, his use of Scripture is less convincing. He insists that Jesus consistently attends and refers in his teaching to meals as 'suppers' rather than 'banquets' (Luke 14:8–14). He is at pains to rule out any invocation of the Christian love-feast or Agape-meal as justification for indulging in a 'a dinner exhaling the odour of the steaming meats and sauces'. Jesus' teaching cannot be twisted to provide a precedent for banquets and receptions that are simply a form of entertainment well removed from the simplicity Jesus envisaged for Christian meals.

More interestingly and persuasively, Clement adapts Paul's teaching about attending meals where food is served that has been offered to idols (1 Corinthians 10:23–11:1). 'The physical act of eating is indifferent' (1 Corinthians 8:8; 9:4; 10:21) notes Clement, but he adds, 'it stands to reason that we forestall passion when we keep pleasures under control' (1 Corinthians 8:9). So, when invited to a neighbour's house, it is not necessary to abstain completely from rich foods, 'but we should not be anxious for them', since we know them to be indifferent. In fact, by restraining from the 'delicacies of the palate', we are practising the kind of virtue that may draw them away from their indulgence. In doing this, we follow the example of Christ (1 Corinthians 11:1). While Clement follows the apostle's argument closely, his language betrays another influence. He tends to translate the principles outlined by Paul into the Stoic categories of 'indifference', 'detachment', and 'self-sufficiency'. These are features of Clement's thought to which we should return.

These pragmatic and Scriptural arguments are set within a framework of clear principle. When they gourmandise, people 'live that they may eat, just like unreasoning beasts; for them life is only their belly'. In contrast, Christ has taught us otherwise: 'our Educator has given the command that we eat only to live. Eating is not our main occupation, nor is pleasure our chief ambition.' Unlike the animals, those who submit to his teaching are being prepared for immortality. And their diet ought to be consistent with his teaching 'plain and ungarnished ... suitable to children who are plain and unpretentious, adapted to maintaining life, not self-indulgence.'

In an age of globalisation, transport, and refrigeration, this is a confronting and challenging perspective. I live on a street with innumerable Thai restaurants, and an assortment of Chinese, Italian, French, Lebanese, Turkish, Indian, African, Norwegian,

Peruvian, and Vietnamese restaurants. And I know what it is like to walk from one end of the street to the other unable to find something to eat. Clement cuts through all this, with his simple advice: 'life depends upon two things only: health and strength. To satisfy these needs, all that is required is a disposition easily satisfied with any sort of food.'

Abuse 2: Excessive consumption of food. The second form of food abuse Clement addressed is gluttony proper, the excessive consumption of food. Gluttony, according to Clement 'is a mania for glutting the appetite, and belly-madness, as the name itself suggests, is lack of self-control with regard to food'. Again, he draws on all his journalistic skills to report what can be found in the Alexandrian eateries of his day in graphic and caustic terms.

> Is it not utterly inane to keep leaning forward from one's couch, all but falling on one's nose into the dishes, as though, according to the common saying, one were leaning out from the nest of the couch to catch the escaping vapours with the nostrils? Is it not completely contrary to reason to keep dipping one's hands into these pastries or to be forever stretching them out for some dish, gorging oneself intemperately and boorishly, not like a person tasting a food, but like one taking it by storm? It is easy to consider such men swine or dogs rather than men, because of their voraciousness.

Hardly a description to leave one's mouth watering.

Having painted the portrait there is not the same need to offer a reasoned critique. Some of his subsequent comments sound more like a handbook of etiquette, advising his readers to keep hands, chin, and couch clean. Decorum dictates that we don't speak while eating, or try to drink and eat at the same time. More substantial is the claim that 'overeating begets in the soul only pain and lethargy and shallow-mindedness'. In terms of Scriptural arguments, Clement refers to Paul's admonishment of the Corinthians' behaviour at the Lord's Supper (1 Corinthians 11:20–22). Clement seems to read this as an indictment of the wealthy who ignored the needs of the poor. They disgrace themselves in a special, two-fold sense: they add to the burden of those without and publicly display their own lack of self-control. The frugality that is consistent with truth can be illustrated from Jesus' diet (John 21:9; Luke 24:41–44; Matthew 17:27); Matthew, who ate seeds, nuts, and herbs; and Peter, who abstained from pork. Surprisingly, John the Baptist escapes censure as a gourmand, despite his exotic diet. This, too, was the intention of the food laws of the Old Testament: to teach frugality.

For Clement, gluttony, like gourmandising, is part of the wider problem of living for pleasure. Food is a matter of indifference (Matthew 15:11), part of God's good provision for his creatures (Matthew 6:26; Job 38:41). Having created the first couple, God declared of all the plants and trees, 'All these things will be food for you' (Genesis 1:29). But abuse of the freedom to enjoy these gifts easily enslaves, reducing us to the level of animals. At his most poetic, Clement expresses his point: 'We ought not to misuse the gifts of the Father, then, acting the part of spendthrifts like the rich son in the Gospel.' He explains:

> They who take advantage of everything that is lawful rapidly
> deteriorate into doing what is unlawful. Just as justice is not
> acquired through covetousness, or temperance through
> licentiousness, so, too, the Christian way of life is not achieved
> by self-indulgence.

These are timely observations for contemporary Christian culture. Does gluttony continue to have a quaint, medieval ring to our ears because of our robust grasp of Christian freedom, or because the blandishments of our world have desensitised us to the snares of self-indulgence and greed? Do we cite the biblical arguments that opened this paper in a desire to discern the will of God, or to rationalise our own luxurious and excessive lifestyles? Do we experience the freedom to eat what we need and choose the occasion to celebrate God's goodness, or are we addicted to consuming simply because we can?

The right use of food

There are many strengths to Clement's treatment of the abuse of food. It is practical, biblical, and colourful. Perhaps its greatest strength is the positive approach offered in the midst of cuttingly sarcastic analysis of the problem. While well able to articulate the abuses of food, he points to its proper use, in keeping with God's loving and lavish intentions in ordering the creation to provide food for his creatures. Food is for sustenance, fellowship, and thanksgiving.

According to Clement, our attitude to food should be informed by recognition that 'life depends upon two things only: health and strength'. So, he advocates a simple and plain diet that 'aids digestion and restricts the weight of the body'. Clement could well have conceived of the advice that is increasingly found on the walls of fruit shops, urging us to have five servings of vegetables and two of fruit each day. He speaks against both overcooking of vegetables and the over-processing of whole grains. And then, as if running the Weight-watchers campaign, he adds: 'We should not overlook the fact, either, that they who dine according to reason, or, rather, according to the Word, are not required to leave sweetmeats and honey out of their fare.'

It would be wrong to simply underline the uncommon sense and prescience of Clement's advice for a culture afflicted with soaring rates of diabetes, obesity, and bowel cancer. His strategy is open to criticism. Living by the word is equivalent to 'life according to reason', the great Stoic ideal. The technology he offers, of detachment from desire by reckoning things indifferent with the goal of self-sufficiency, despite a superficial resonance with Christian categories, is ultimately alien to the resources Paul offers in the gospel and the Spirit of the living God. Clement prefers a type of asceticism, although his biblical faithfulness keeps him from excesses in this regard.

This tendency is most apparent in Clement's muted endorsement of fellowship as an intended function of eating. 1 Corinthians 11 highlights the tragic destruction of fellowship by selfishness. Part of the horror of gluttony is the isolation it brings, as the person preoccupied with food withdraws from those around. 'Lavishness is not capable of being enjoyed alone', observes Clement, 'it must be bestowed on others.' Conversely, the Christian should share in the meal provided at the neighbour's house, even if rich foods are on the menu, out of 'respect for him who has invited us and not to lessen or destroy the sociability of the gathering'. However, he shows little enthusiasm for the banquet, only begrudgingly allowing, '[f]estive gatherings of themselves do contain some spark of love, for from food taken at a common table we become accustomed to the food of eternity.'

It seems that, confronted by the excesses of his day, Clement underestimates the value of meals and of celebrations. This is hard to square with the emphasis on table-fellowship in Jesus' ministry and his participation in festive celebrations. Jesus shows that it is possible to participate in these without succumbing to self-indulgence. In his emphasis on the heavenly banquet as the goal of the Christian, Clement tends to despise the present material world in favour of that spiritual reality.

Yet, Clement's emphasis is a welcome one. For him, 'the true food is thanksgiving'. This is the corollary of the fact that we do 'not live by bread alone' (Matthew 4:4). It is thanksgiving that keeps raising the eyes from the horizon of the table to the hand that provides, and will set the not-yet banquet table. And it is thanksgiving that offers protection from the temptations of the table now, because 'he who always offers up thanks will not indulge excessively in pleasure.'

Is food the new sex? Yes and no. The human heart will always find a way to manufacture idols, and the belly provides a range of options. Just as a generation has taken the good gift of sexual expression and abused it, seeking new, more exotic experiences, assuming that nothing exceeds like excess, and still can find no real satisfaction, it will find a way to do the same with food. But the 'new sex'? Clement reminds us there is nothing new under the sun.

ENDNOTES

1. I am delighted to dedicate these gratuitous references to cricket and sex to my former teacher, colleague, and batting partner, Michael Hill.

2. www20.sbs.com.au/heatinthekitchen/index: 'In the current era, where food is the new sex and chefs have become the new rock stars food critics have a powerful role in creating or destroying these new celebrities and their livelihoods.'

3. It represents a variation on the fashion dictum that 'x (insert colour) is the new black'. For reasons I won't elaborate, I am more drawn to the suggestion that '50 is the new 40'.

4. Cathy von Kintzel, 'Food is the new sex: Media attention on body image, eating choices has made sex boring, professor says', The Halifax Herald, Friday September 30, 2005.

5. Felipe Fernandez-Armesto, The Guardian, September 14, 2002.

6. All biblical quotes in this chapter are taken from the NRSV, unless indicated otherwise.

7. Most authors cite this quote. E.g., H. Fairlie, The Seven Deadly Sins, (Notre Dame: University of Notre Dame Press, 1978), 107.

8. Anthony Campolo, Seven Deadly Sins, (Condell Park: Christian Press, 1987), 109.

9. Campolo, Seven, 112, 'There is little justification for the humiliation which so many must suffer at the hands of insensitive and uninformed preachers who like to wax prophetic at the expense of people who are already suffering in ways that are not readily understood.'

10. Mary Louise Bringle, *The God of Thinness: Gluttony and Other Weighty Matters* (Nashville, Abingdon, 1992), 109.
11. Bringle, *The God of Thinness,* 116.
12. A proper discussion of the complex relationship between attacks on obesity and the encouragement of eating disorders such as anorexia and bulimia is beyond the scope of this paper and my competence. For an informative introduction to the issues, see S. Abrahams and D. Llewellyn-Jones, *Eating Disorders: The Facts* (3rd ed.; Oxford: Oxford University Press, 1992), 28–39.
13. Clement of Alexandria, *Stromateis,* 6.9.
14. H. B. Swete, *Patristic Study* (London: MacMillan, 1902), 48.
15. Cited in E. Molland, *The Conception of the Gospel in the Alexandrian Theology* (Oslo, 1938).
16. This translates the Greek title, *Paidagōgus*. The first and last paragraphs of book 2, chapter 1 (1, 18) cite the verse. All quotations from this text are taken from, *The Fathers of the Church: Clement of Alexandria: Christ the Educator* (Tr. Simon Wood; Washington: Catholic University of America Press, 1954). Chapter 2 addresses the problem of excessive drinking and alcohol abuse. Since this raises so many distinctive issues, the focus of this paper is chapter one's treatment of food.

STILL DEADLY

AQUINAS ON ANGER
GORDON PREECE

Do you secretly enjoy moments of anger? After all, to be in that moment of anger is to feel powerful, in control, and absolutely *right*. Perhaps your enjoyment of those moments is not even a secret. You think your anger is normal and natural, and when others complain, you say 'this is just who I am' and advise them to back off.

Yet our society notices angry people: Manchester United's fiery Wayne Rooney was sent to an 'anger management' course for his many angry outbursts. Our society also marvels at the folly of anger: Zinedine Zidane's infamous head-butt to Italian Marco Materazzi during the 2006 World Cup final was a moment that many said ruined an otherwise brilliant career. Increasingly anger is associated with ill health: as Ruth Ostrow notes in *The Australian* magazine, 'anger is worse for our immunity and wellbeing than anything we can ingest. Anger is internally and spiritually corrosive in a way that no chocolate bar could ever be'.[1]

So what do you make of your anger? You may have seen the evils of uncontrolled anger, and in response, you think that *every* expression of anger is evil. Although anger boils within you, you try never to express it.

A preacher once told this story of a woman who visited a counsellor and explained how much anger and hatred she felt toward her husband. She wanted to leave him. The counsellor suggested the best revenge: she should go home, pretend to be very loving, grant his every wish—and then when he was completely besotted, leave. The woman went home and followed his advice out of sheer will power, but she fell back in love with her husband, and they lived happily ever after. The preacher used the story to illustrate his view that anger can and should be switched off by force of will. But does our will rule anger in this way?

We remain ambivalent about anger. We are strangely drawn to its strength, yet repelled by its excesses. We are attracted to its outbursts, and drawn to stories about those who master it. For all our society's advances, anger leaves us a bit mystified.

It is appropriate and important, then, to arrange our own 'anger management' class with 'the angelic doctor', Thomas Aquinas. This great thirteenth-century Christian thinker offers an 'anatomy' of anger that retains enduring appeal. His account is more 'philosophical' than we are used to, and he tends to use biblical passages in an illustrative way. He argues from our design and purpose to show how our anger springs from thwarted desires and threatened loves. His account is a kind of *How and Why of Anger*. It is found in his monumental *Summa Theologiae* [ST].[2]

Anger and the logic of emotion

Aquinas seeks to unpack and understand the complex inter-connected springs of human emotion as part of the whole person in God's world. Anger is an emotion, and to understand it we need to understand the general and God-given role of human emotions. Humans are social, 'relational' creatures, and therefore anger cannot be viewed in an isolated, individualistic way. As Catholic philosopher Tom Ryan notes of an emotion:

> Its significance can only be fully appreciated through its interconnection with other human powers, with the total person especially as under the guidance of reason, with others, the world, and, most importantly, with God. For Aquinas, within his teleological [or purpose-driven] view of the person, emotions are integral to human functioning, growth and moral integration.

When our emotions go awry, we go awry. Our emotions need ordering, and for Thomas Aquinas 'it is love for God that plays this role: "all our passions can be ordered by this passion for God".'[3] But that is a very general claim, so Aquinas gives more detail about how he thinks emotions work, and how a 'passion for God' brings order to wayward emotions. In what follows, I outline Aquinas' account of anger by making ongoing reference to his theological and philosophical perspective on emotions.

Aquinas noticed the way emotions 'move' us. He defines an emotion as an immediate or spontaneous movement, or a physical or affectionate response to a particular object or purpose (ST I.II.22.2–3). But they are not just involuntary, animal-like, instinctive reactions to a stimulus, as when rats get food or an electric shock. For Aquinas, an emotion like anger is a form of *rational, intentional human awareness*. It is something we can control responsibly. But Aquinas carefully qualifies this account.

A common pop-psychology excuse for anger is that it is 'just the way I feel, I can't help it'. But while an emotion can be passive in this way (as when I am negatively 'moved' or made angry by an act upon me like an insult), it can also be active (as when I move to or from something because of its attractive or repelling power, its value or disvalue, such as returning the insult with interest). This interplay of passive and active, being moved and moving is due to our organic, unified nature as embodied, rational souls, and to our relational nature interacting with others. There is also interplay between these aspects of ourselves, and the degree to which we share a passion for God.

It is central to Aquinas' psychology that humans are distinctively rational animals even though this capacity isn't perfectly developed or applied (ST I.2.46.5)—especially when we're angry! Yet from the start (ST I.II.24.1–2) Aquinas clearly rejects the ancient Stoics (for example, Cicero's) rationalist view of emotions as evil or diseased. Unlike the Stoics, and like Aristotle, he sees that emotions are rational and human 'to the extent ... they share in the life of reason'. To that extent they are not 'diseases' or 'disturbances of the soul' (seen as purely invisible and intellectual). Therefore emotions can be moderate or immoderate, ethically good or bad.

This more holistic and intimate view of the relation between reason and emotion contrasts with the common mechanical Divine Command ethic known as voluntarism or 'will-power religion'. Thoughts trickle down over time transforming our emotions, and so there is a half-truth embedded in the preacher's illustration about the will power of the woman who wanted to leave her husband. God's command to love is not mere advice for when we feel like it. It involves the mind and will. The early Aquinas thought the will was moved purely by reason, and that to habitually follow the mind and will changes our character.

But there is no simple one-way or trickle-down relationship from reason and will to emotion, as in the non-Christian view of the Stoics. Later (ST I.II.9.1; 9.1 ad 3), Aquinas saw *four* factors converging in any free human choice. It is true that will is moved by reason; but our bodily passions also influence the way a desirable or undesirable object is presented to the will. In addition, the will is moved by its object or goal, and also by God.[4] Such complexity is reflected in the Great Commandment to love

God 'with all our heart, soul, mind and strength': such love is profoundly affective or emotional love, and is grounded in our embodiment ('strength'). (This more complex account is also found in Jonathon Edwards' *Religious Affections* and Michael Hill's *The How and Why of Love*.)

BIOGRAPHY OF THOMAS AQUINAS

Thomas Aquinas was born in 1225, the youngest son of a knight, near Aquino, 50 miles north-west of Naples in Italy. He began school in 1230 at the magnificent Montecassino Benedictine monastery. In 1239 he entered Naples University and then at 19 joined the Dominican preaching order founded by Dominic de Guzman to preach against the heretical dualistic and ascetic Cathar sect. However, his family, set on a lucrative church career with the Benedictines, imprisoned him for a year. Released in 1245 Thomas followed the Dominican polymath Albert the Great to study in Paris and then in 1248 in Cologne at a time of great renewal of learning and new universities among Jews (Maimonides), Muslims (Averroes) and Christians. The Dominicans sought to secure the new universities for the Church against heresies. But they out-thought, not out-fought them. Though it was during the Crusades, Aquinas hardly mentions them. Fellow-students called Aquinas 'The Dumb Ox', maybe more a comment on his temperament and portly physique than his intellect. He was said to never be angry except when he threw out a woman planted in his room to lead him to sin.

Further study in Paris was followed by teaching in Italy using the dialogical disputations or question and answer method. This posed a question, quoted the best mutually accepted authorities, for and against his particular perspective, including 10,000 objections in *Summa Theologiae*, and sought a higher synthesis. Disputation was an intellectual way of disciplining oneself to play the ball not the man, to engage in precise, friendly argument, not aimless anger. For the means had to correspond to the end, friendship with God.

After his *Summa Contra Gentiles* he wrote his magnum opus *Summa Theologica*, using this method from 1260 until 1273 when he suddenly stopped after a heavenly vision, feeling there was no more to say. He died the next year. In 1278 his teaching became official Dominican teaching. He was recognised as a doctor of the church in the 19th century.

When we listen to Aquinas' two *Summas* we eavesdrop on a vast conversation across the centuries. He sought to reconcile the dominant theology of Augustine with the newly rediscovered philosophy of Aristotle. Aquinas produced the most complete summary of Christian belief to that day, and some still say, to today. He wrote over eight and a half million words of tightly disciplined argument. He considered all areas of thought his domain—politics, law, economics, and psychology, despite the limitations of living before the age of empirical science. He understood 'how quite different sciences can converge on the same conclusion by different arguments and data'.[5] Yet through it all we see Thomas in conversation with Christ the teacher of a new wisdom correcting and completing the science and wisdom of the world.

Aquinas' anatomy of emotion

Tom Ryan usefully unpacks Aquinas' subtle understanding of persons, emotions and ethics.

1. What is 'rationally "fitting" ... with a holistic human nature mediates the emotional virtues (faith, hope and love) as they structure our specific emotional responses (anger)'. Our bodily desires or passions are moved by something, real or imagined, seen as helpful or harmful to our whole human nature. Our rational desire or will is moved not by bare knowledge, but by the truth seen as a good and desirable object. 'It is the practical intellect, not the speculative intellect that moves the will'.[6]

The basis of an emotion being 'fitting' is Aquinas' teleological biblical and philosophical framework. An act or emotion is good when our reason finds it fitting or appropriate to achieve the goal of a fully functioning, flourishing human life. As we move toward that goal, we become more fully human and virtuous; as we move away from it we become less human (ST I.II.22.1 and ad 3). Over time, by habit and through grace, we become more human and happier or blessed. We seek not only what is good universally, but also what is good particularly for us, in terms of what we are passionate about. But if something is a threat to what we are passionate about, it arouses our anger.

Emotions move or arouse our will by the way they fit or deflect from our goal of living a whole human life. Hence just as we commonly use the term 'emotional literacy' today, so we can speak of 'emotional fitness'. Fitness is general or universal in terms of our goal or value of leading a long healthy life. But it is also specific, judged according to our specific sporting goal. The flexible fitness of a young gymnast is different to the strength fitness of a mature weight lifter. Similarly, in a particular case an emotion like anger can be seen as being good or fitting, or evil or unfitting, in terms of our general or specific emotional fitness.

For someone who is angry, something can seem good or valuable when he or she is agitated that is not so when they are calm (cf ST I.II.9.2). A friend was waiting with blinker on and legitimately took a parking spot when it became vacant. But another woman had not seen her, and suddenly my friend was on the receiving end of this woman's road rage, because of her perception that she'd unjustly lost a precious parking spot after looking long and hard. She followed my friend and abused her for quite a while holding up traffic. Later, the other driver might well have wondered why she lost her cool. Through an over-valued object (the parking place), the exhausted and misperceiving emotion moved the will in the wrong direction—a direction not fitting with wholeness or peace.

2. Aquinas evaluates emotions such as anger according to how fitting or in tune they are with a voluntary and rightly directed reason.[7] Even if an act (such as abusing my friend in the parking lot) isn't accomplished, the wilful readiness to do so is wrong (even if, for example, the abusive woman was distracted by another space becoming available) (ST I.II.17.4; I.II.20.3). Compare Jesus' challenging correlation of act and intention: 'You have heard that it was said to the people long ago, "Do not murder and anyone who murders will be subject to judgment." But I tell you that anyone who is angry with his brother will be subject to judgment. Again, anyone who says to his brother, *Raca*, is answerable to the Sanhedrin. But anyone who says, "You fool!" will be in danger of the fire of hell' (Matthew 5:21–22).

Aquinas also sees emotions like anger as revealing the underlying beliefs that are integral to our habitual attitudes. These emotions 'have a formative influence'[8] on our own and others' character. They form an 'attitude arsenal' ready for future action. The habitually angry person develops an angry character through feedback from their actions. (While sometimes I think I'd like to become an 'angry old man' like Bob Geldof, I'm not sure that my anger with my computer or a poor driver is as good a cause as eliminating world poverty.)

3. Aquinas spotlights 'the psychological and physical resonance of emotions in moral living'. In ST I.II.24.3, he sees emotion as adding to or detracting from the goodness or evil of an act. Firstly, an emotion's overflowing intensity (anger at poverty) comes from the will's desire for goodness, and is a sign of its greater worth. Hence Jesus' righteous and zealous anger against the misuse of God's house consumes him when cleansing the temple (John 2:17). Secondly, when an emotion resonates with the will's choice of the good, it reverberates psychologically and physically and *enables and reinforces* the ethical aspect of the act. These echoes profoundly affect the whole person and their rational, wilful and emotional powers, 'in a form of organic synergy'.[9] However, without the perfection of Jesus' fully human and divine anger shown in John 2, organic synergy can easily tilt over into an orgy of sin.

4. Using a political master-metaphor of the *polis* (city), Aquinas captures the intimate mutual learning and interdependence of mind, will and emotions in everyday practical reasoning. Humans are like mini-city states governed by political persuasion, not by despotic dictation. Reason rules the emotions by 'persuasion and coordination'—a very different account than Plato and neo-Platonism's dualistic and autocratic picture of reason's rule over emotion. Plato's *Republic* 'portrays reason as the helmsman of the soul and the ship of state, beleaguered by the motley crew of rebellious passions'.[10] There are many Christian Platonists still around, and Aquinas' concept of the human as a miniature political community shows why the preacher's claim about the power of willpower over emotion was, in the final analysis, wrong.

Instead, for Aquinas the *heart* or *imagination* is the mediating or integrating point of the person (ST I.II.24.2 ad 2 and 37.4). Emotions, unlike bodily movements directly controlled by reason, are subject to *indirect* control by reason via the will.

Emotions have relative freedom to cooperate or conquer. But at their best, 'emotions and reason tutor each other' symbiotically. 'It is the role of the virtues [faith, hope and love leavening self-control, courage, justice and prudence] to guide the emotion, to overcome any resistance' but without suppressing its energy and power.[11]

This two-way movement can be illustrated by angry responses to injustice. It is not only compassion for refugees and their children that has aroused many Australians and Christians to protest our government's mandatory detention policies. It is also righteous anger. Anger can be a strong motivating force for social justice and change, rousing reason from its slumber and from what Martin Luther King called 'the paralysis of analysis'.

Reason is also necessary to restrain anger. It was needed in late November 2006 to restrain the anarchic anger of the white plastic-suited group of anti-G20 protestors in Melbourne, who distracted from the reasoned response of many other protesters, and in effect the G20 Finance Ministers, were let off lightly.

5. In Aquinas' innovative, integrated view of humans, emotions are located within a holistic intersecting matrix of body, reason and will all ordered by a passion for God and by habitual virtues. Hence for Aquinas, the body is not 'the prison-house of the soul' as in Plato's dualism. Closer to Aristotle and the Bible, he sees the body as the *integral form* of the soul, or the soul as the whole human person. For Aquinas, virtue does not lie in the superior realm of the spirit, above the emotions and body. Instead our passions, including righteous anger, are an overflowing of the energies and fruit (virtues) of the human and divine Spirit. Our emotions, including anger, can be gradually transformed into a fitting expression of our full humanity so that we respond to the good 'with greater promptness, ease and joy'.[12] In Aquinas we see a truly Christian form of 'emotional intelligence' that long anticipates Daniel Goleman's 1996 book of the same name. For Aquinas, such emotional intelligence or virtue or literacy is a key way in which we

read and act out the story of salvation, with its ultimate goal in eternal, friendly contemplation of a relational God.

The affective virtues habituate us to feel compassionate, angry, afraid, loving, sad, joyful about the right things, at the right time and to the right degree. The cardinal 'affective' virtues (whether described as fortitude and temperance or fidelity and self-care) shape, guide and moderate our emotional responses with regard to oneself, others and God. Our emotions provide both the threads and the colour to the tapestry of our lives.[13]

Aquinas' anatomy of anger

So far I have presented Aquinas' view of anger as interwoven with his wider account of emotion. But Aquinas also examines the nature, causes and effects of anger. Unfortunately, we cannot examine this dense material in detail, but I will offer a few summary highlights (found in ST I.II.46–48), with some modern reflections.

Aquinas thinks that emotions are broadly of two types—the 'concupiscible' and the 'irascible'. 'Concupiscible' emotions straightforwardly desire good (love) or flee evil (hatred). But 'irascible' emotions are about our enduring difficulty in overcoming obstacles on our journey to good and away from evil (I. 81.2; I.II.23.1).[14]

Anger is irascible. It is a spirited emotion that faces difficulty by hitting back at evil, imposing punishment or wreaking revenge upon its cause. So anger is often aroused by other emotions, such as sorrow at a loss (and so according to Elisabeth Kubler Ross's stages of grief, anger appears after denial and bargaining, and before acceptance). Or anger can be due to hope denied (for victory in sport or promotion at work). In this way it is a complex emotion, and is always deeply interwoven with one or several other emotions.

It is closely related to our sense of justice and injustice. The hurtful or harmful thing arousing our anger is seen as an injustice, and the person suffering the injustice wants to right it by restoring justice or enacting punishment. But sadly, anger is so upsetting that it unbalances our reason, obstructing us from making right judgments. Reason after the Fall is often rationalisation and self-justification (Romans 1:21–22, 28, 32). Aquinas is sometimes too optimistic about reason, seeing us as *deprived* of supernatural grace by our fall into sin but not totally *depraved* (by which Reformed theologians mean that the Fall affects our every part including our reason, not that all people are as bad as people can possibly be). However when it comes to anger, Aquinas is more realistic. Anger distorts our perceptions and reason.

Anger seeks satisfaction or pleasure (a good) by defending itself against whatever afflicts, arouses or obstructs it (an evil). But this pleasure can take an evil form: thoughts of vengeance can be caressed as lovingly as a lover's body. And acting out one's vengeance also pleases us, because we see it as the righting of a wrong. This is especially the case when some wrong to us is obvious—as in the case of 'unmerited contempt'. Being belittled by someone we see as petty or lacking something adds fuel to our fire. So an accomplished preacher or singer 'is more quickly and bitterly incensed against an ignoramus offering insult than against an educated and experienced man whose opinion of good speaking or singing has presumably a claim to a hearing'. But the person who says sorry dispels anger more quickly and completely than the apology of someone who should know better. If God overlooks ignorance (Acts 17:30) and cools his anger, perhaps we should also be more willing to do so. Is it then biblically legitimate to experience pleasure at contemplating vengeance? According to Romans 12:19 and 21, we should, 'leave room for God's wrath ... do not be overcome by evil, but overcome evil with good'. Rather than nursing and acting out our anger, we find God's anger to be the truest and best defence of our God-given value.

Anger affects the body more than other emotions, stirring it to act forcefully, impetuously, and vehemently. We do well to notice the bodily symptoms of our anger, which may in turn give us a chance either to control them (counting to ten, deep breathing, praying) or to decide whether this is one of those rare moments when it is right that we should be stirred to action.

But it can also be seen in the surly silence of a taciturn nature.[15] Many Australians are men of few words, but a slow burn goes on within. Australians often seem to bear an invisible anger at the tough land they inherited. Further, the pervasiveness of often inhumanly paced technology leads to a kind of technological taciturnity that bursts out in road rage, rage against machines, and referees in all sports. Aquinas notes that being taciturn may save us from sins of angry speech. At least being taciturn or sullenly silent saves one from 'inordinate speech', the inability to shut up, illustrating Proverbs 25:28 'Like a city whose walls are broken down is a man who lacks self control'. I find myself wondering how we might find a right balance between taciturnity, and properly voicing our anger so that it does not burst out uncontrollably.

Aquinas asks whether anger is more serious than hatred. He answers that while anger can be more intense than hatred (citing Proverbs 27:4), it is not as long-lasting. It is more reasonable and more easily mollified by satisfying its quest for justice. Aquinas' great theological authority, Augustine, uses Jesus' figure of speech (Luke 6:41–42) to see anger as the 'speck of sawdust', and hatred as the 'plank' in the eye of passion. This is why Ephesians 4:26–27 quotes Psalm 4:4 "In your anger do not sin" [or hate]: 'Do not let the sun go down while you are still angry, and do not give the devil a foothold'.

Learning to handle anger

Anger is not strictly evil or a vice. We can be angry without sinning, as Jesus did and as God does, although that is not easy. Anger is not devilish in itself, but becomes so when fed and held on to so it grows to become hatred. To 'maintain the rage' is the real problem that leads to hatred or sin. What makes anger sinful is loss of truthful rational and relational awareness and communication and a sense of proportion (hence Ephesians 4:25, 'each of you must put off falsehood and speak truthfully to his neighbour, for we are all members of one body'.) To adapt Luther's colourful illustration about temptation: 'you can't help a bird landing on your head, but you can stop it building a nest'.

How can we handle our anger? Peter Fitzsimon's story of the newly converted Australian rugby captain Nick Farr-Jones provides a good example. Fitzsimons, who is often sceptical of Christian sportsmen, writes with grudging respect for Farr-Jones:

> Farr-Jones' family credit Christianity with giving him a more rounded, gentler view of the world, and with helping to curb his explosive temper. While once he might have tended to explode immediately into a rage over the smallest thing, they could almost see him mentally consulting the Christian texts before flying off the handle.

Fitzsimons also recounts a story told by Nick's mate Simon, about when they and some friends went to the Caringbah local for 'a bit of a drink' a couple of years after Nick's conversion to Christ.

> 'We were all sitting at the table, having a beer, and these guys were sitting next to us, drinking heavily, becoming more and more drunk, and they started sliding their empty beer glasses across the table and smashing them into ours,' said Simon. 'As soon as this started you could see the look in Nick's eyes ... I thought, 'oh, no, he's going to blow', but it seemed his new

Christianity was holding him back. And he just said to one of the guys, 'Don't do that. Please don't do that again'. So these guys thought that was great and the next guy finishes his glass and slides it across and it smashes a glass right next to Nick on the table. So Nick jumps out of his seat, grabs the guy, hurls him against the wall and says, 'Listen, mate, I'm a Christian first but I'm getting very angry and if you do that again I'll kill you'.

The guy just got back into his chair like he was scared stiff and we didn't hear a word from them for the rest of the evening'.[16]

While far from perfect, this response was not bad for a two year-old Christian with a bad temper, and is a wonderful example of 'muscular Christianity'. Farr-Jones felt the pull of anger, even righteous anger, but he felt the stronger pull of God's Word and Spirit giving him rational self-control which moderated the way he expressed his anger.

Aquinas provides only scattered suggestions for dealing with anger, and then only in reference to the main motive or root cause of anger—suffering an injury or insult (ST I.II.47). One remedy is to diminish the tormenting, aggravating thought by any means available. Distraction is a great thing, but the positive distraction of reflecting on God's gracious 'slow to anger' character through Scripture, worship and prayer is even better. Good company, good wine and stepping outside and smelling the roses don't hurt either. I have often found after fighting with my wife on the way to visiting someone that enjoyable relationships with others reduces the issue to its true proportions. I particularly remember once arguing while driving with my son and being very angry until we saw a nude psychiatric patient, wearing only runners, and both laughing so much we forgot what we were angry about.

Aquinas notes that friends can hurt or fail us more than others and arouse greater anger. As Psalm 55:12 says 'if an enemy were insulting me, I could endure it'. Anger can fracture friendships but appropriate anger, well received by a gentle answer, can strengthen them. 'A gentle answer turns away wrath, but a harsh word stirs up anger' (Proverbs 15:1). Can we become better at cultivating gentle answers as an antidote to anger? Intense anger can lead to foolishness (ST II.II.41.2–3). The animalistic threat of such anger to our human reason requires the mitigating effect of meekness or gentleness (ST II.II.157.4). When we are dismayed at our ongoing anger, we should remember Moses' anger management problems, which led him to kill, albeit in defence of justice to Israelite slaves (Exodus 2:11–12). But this same Moses later became known as 'the meekest man in all the earth'. How can the blessing of meekness and the hope of inheriting the earth (Matthew 5:5) help us deal with anger?

Scripture's gentle command is 'Do not let the sun go down while you are still angry, and do not give the devil a foothold' (Ephesians 4:26). This has been standard pre-marital pastoral advice. Misunderstandings inevitably happen and we are most hurt by the ones we love most. Keep short accounts: 'Love keeps no record of wrongs' (1 Corinthians 13:5). Married people can begin to sort it out with some pillow talk, and maybe a bit more. 'Get rid of all bitterness, rage and anger, brawling and slander, along with every form of malice. Be kind and compassionate to one another, forgiving each other, just as in Christ God forgave you' (Ephesians 4:31–32). Keeping the forgiveness we have received from Christ first and foremost in our minds and hearts puts the fun back into marriage and relationships generally.

Aquinas' explanation of the emotions is more philosophical and causal in form than biblical. It is not anti-biblical, but biblical passages are more illustrative than constitutive. If in relation to the cosmic, objective world Aquinas uses an Aristotelian argument from design and causality to demonstrate the origin of the universe in the existence of God, so in relation to the human, subjective world he uses an Aristotelian argument from desire or desire thwarted, to trace the origin of anger in love thwarted. For Aquinas our external and inner world is an infinite and intricate chain of causes going all the way back to God. Aquinas seeks to unpack and understand the complex inter-connected springs of human emotion as part of the whole person in God's world. This orientation to God's love as our compass and all-encompassing reality is fundamentally biblical though less explicitly biblically-shaped than Michael Hill's *The How and Why of Love*. Aquinas has much to teach us about anger, just as Michael Hill has much to teach us about love. Michael may retire formally from his work, with our best wishes, but he will never retire from the work of loving relationships.

ENDNOTES

1. Ruth Ostrow, *The Weekend Australian*, Saturday May 20, 2006; Online: www.ruthostrow.com/wozmag060520.pdf.

2. *Summa Theologiae* [ST], Latin text and English Dominican Fathers translation (Blackfriars with Eyre & Spottiswoode: London), 1963–75.

3. Tom Ryan, 'Aquinas' Integrated View of Emotions, Morality and the Person', *Pacifica* 14 (February 2001), 58 citing G. Simon Harak, *Virtuous Passions: The Formation of Christian Character* (Paulist: Mahwah, NJ: 1993), 77, commenting on Thomas Aquinas, S.T. I. II. 28.5.

4. J-P. Torrell, *Saint Thomas Aquinas: Vol 1: The Person and His Work* (Catholic University Press of America: Washington DC, 1996), 245.

5. John Finnis, *Aquinas: Moral, Political and Legal Theory* (Oxford University Press: Oxford: 1998), 7, 4.

6. Ryan, 59 citing ST I.II.91 ad 2.

7. Ryan, 61.

8. Ryan, 62–3.

9. Ibid.

10. W.C. Spohn, 'Passions and Principles', in 'Notes on Moral Theology 1990', *Theological Studies* 52 (1991) p. 70 cited in Ryan, p. 65.

11. Ryan, 65.

12. Ryan, 66–7.

13. Ryan, 69.

14. While the distinction between irascible passions and concupiscible desires

is disputed there are analogies in Plato's division of the soul into 'desiring' (cf concupiscence) and 'spirited' (cf irascibility) parts and Freud's contrast between 'erotic' and 'aggressive' instincts (Kevin White, commentary on ST, 'The Passions of the Soul', IaIIae, qq. 22–48, 109).

15. I owe much of the summary of this section on anger to Paul J Glenn, *A Tour of the Summa* (Tan Books: Rockford Ill, 1960), 44–47.

16. Peter Fitzsimons, *Nick Farr-Jones: the authorised biography* (Random House; Milson's Point, 1994), 46.

REINHOLD NIEBUHR ON PRIDE
GRAHAM COLE

What are you proud of?

We 'swell up' with pride for many reasons—when we look in the mirror, or review our trophy cabinet, or remember our successes at work, college or university. We can be proud of others: that we have raised them as our children, or that they have performed well for our organisation or nation, or even simply that we know them. We can feel pride simply because we are glad to be members of some group, not only because we enjoy the group's benefits, but sometimes also because we think that we and the others who comprise it are somehow better than others.

Complex thoughts and feelings are associated with 'pride', yet it has long been thought to have a dark side. Prometheus is that character in ancient Greek mythology who defied the gods, and so the term 'Promethean' has come to be used of excessive pride. In the Christian tradition, pride has been typically viewed as the worst of the seven deadly sins.[1] For example Dante, in his medieval masterpiece *The Divine Comedy*, presents pride as the root of all sin and therefore the lowest level of purgatory from which one must ascend. Once pride has been beaten, suggests Dante, being purified of the other six sins becomes easier.[2]

But has this ancient concern about the dark side of pride been overstated? After all in the modern West it is taken as a basic truth that we must 'have pride in ourselves'. This claim is taught in elementary schools, in daytime self-help television, and in many Hollywood movies. 'National pride', 'gay pride', 'pride in the corporation' and 'family pride' are just some of the 'prides' that arise from time to time.

Why should we look to a mid-century American theologian for help? Simply because Reinhold Niebuhr took human sin seriously, and understood the human problem at its deepest level. James O. Freedman, president emeritus of Dartmouth College and the University of Iowa, describes the impact of this aspect of Niebuhr's ideas on his own life: 'Niebuhr's views appealed to me because they seemed true. They recognised the manner in which hubris [arrogant pride] infects human action, most especially when men and women "try to play God in history".'[3]

Niebuhr's account of pride

Niebuhr's views on pride were formed as he was taught by his Bible, the witness of great Christians of the past such as Augustine and Kierkegaard, and through experience as well. It was when Niebuhr began work in a poor parish in Detroit that he saw human sin at its most raw, especially in its effects on workers in the auto industry there. In particular, as a pastor he tried to comfort those who were dying. Two such affected him deeply. Both were church members. One lady was 'preoccupied with self' and 'in a constant hysteria of fear and resentment'. The other 'expressed gratitude for all the mercies of God which she had received in life'. Niebuhr movingly recounts: 'I relearned the essentials of the Christian faith at the bedside of that nice old soul. I appreciated that the ultimate problem of human existence is the peril of sin and death.'[4] He also saw 'the mystery of grace' in their very different responses to dying. The shallowness of the theological liberalism of his day, with its optimism about human nature, was revealed by such experiences. He also came to see that the faith of modern man in progress and human perfectibility was based on a view of human nature that was far inferior to what he called 'the Biblical view of man' in all its realism.[5]

Although Niebuhr did not use the seven deadly sins as an organising schema, like Dante he saw pride as the fundamental sin. According to Niebuhr pride is humanity's 'basic sin', 'sin in its quintessential form', and 'the very essence of human sin'.[6] Pride is placing one's ego at the centre of existence, and it manifests itself in rebellion towards God (a religious category) and injustice towards others (a moral category).[7] It is the sin of the devil, as seen when the prophet who has been speaking of the pride of ancient Babylon then goes on to speak of the arch-enemy of God:

How you are fallen from heaven, O Lucifer, son of the morning!
How you are cut down to the ground, you who weakened the nations!
For you have said in your heart: 'I will ascend into heaven,
I will exalt my throne above the stars of God ...'
(Isaiah 14:12–13, New KJV)[8]

Niebuhr understood the Genesis story as a myth to be taken seriously (but not literally). There, the root of Adam's sin was unbelief in the goodness of God and a tragic belief in the serpent's false interpretation of God's command, which cast suspicion on God's goodness and successfully tempted man to think that he could 'break and transcend the limits God has set for him.'[9]

Niebuhr was aware that 'the definition of sin as pride' had a long and consistent history in Christian thought. He quotes from Augustine, Pascal, Luther, Thomas Aquinas and Calvin as evidence.[10] Niebuhr's analysis of pride is worth revisiting because of its sophistication. He wrote:

> It will be convenient in this analysis to distinguish between three types of pride, which are, however, never completely distinct in actual life: pride of power, pride of knowledge and pride of virtue. The third type, the pride of self-righteousness, rises to a form of spiritual pride, which is at once a fourth type and yet not a specific form of pride at all but pride and self-glorification in its inclusiveness and quintessential form.[11]

The 'pride of power' shows itself when the human ego attempts to surmount its creaturely limitations. If the ego feels secure it forgets its limitations and the impending judgment of God.[12] If the ego feels insecure it seeks to be secure at the expense of others, including nature. Greed is an expression of such insecure pride. In both cases, the proud ego uses the will-to-power to serve its goals.[13]

The 'pride of knowledge' shows itself in the intellectual who believes he or she has final truth: 'Each great thinker makes the same mistake, in turn, of imagining himself the final thinker.'[14] The thinker cannot see the limitations in his or her perspective. Niebuhr thought that the Marxist thinkers of his day fell into this kind of pride.[15]

The 'pride of virtue', or moral pride, is that self-righteousness which occurs '[w]hen the self mistakes its standards for God's standards.'[16] This kind of pride becomes spiritual pride and the ultimate sin of self-deification when it identifies its 'partial and relative attainments' with 'the unconditioned good, and claims divine sanction.'[17] This is the pride that persecutes others.

Niebuhr not only saw sin as a problem for each individual. He also saw it as a major problem within groups, and an example of collective sin. He wrote: 'A distinction between group pride and the egotism of individuals is necessary ... because the pretensions and claims of a collective or social self exceed those of the individual ego.'[18]

> Collective pride is thus man's last, and in some respects most pathetic, effort to deny the determinate and contingent character of his existence. The very essence of human sin is in it. It can hardly be surprising that this form of human sin is also the most fruitful of human guilt, that is of objective social and historical evil. In its whole range from pride of family to pride of nations, collective egotism and group pride are a more pregnant source of injustice and conflict than purely individual pride.[19]

Nations may deify themselves; the prophets of Israel preached against her attempt to do just that;[20] and Niebuhr thought that the Nazis of his day had fallen into this sin.[21] Importantly then, Niebuhr did not make the mistake of privatising sin as though it were only a religious problem of the individual before God.

Niebuhr critiqued

According to William John Wolf, by making pride the basic sin Niebuhr fails 'to account for the sins of the weak man. This failure to be the man needs to be included in the Niebuhrian topography of sin.'[22] Not all of us are Prometheus-like. In fact, in the Genesis narrative Adam and Eve hide from God (Genesis 3:8). Moreover, Wolf maintains, although Niebuhr regards 'unbelief or faithlessness as the essential root of sin' he fails to develop this insight to account for those 'human perversities quite inadequately explained by 'pride.'[23] Wolf's point is a fair one.

More recently feminist theologians have contended that there are inadequacies in Niebuhr's account of sin. Daphne Hampson argues that Niebuhr's story of pride as the basic sin is true of males, but not of females. She does not believe that

Niebuhr's analysis is false. In fact she lauds it. Rather, her complaint is that it is so male. She writes: 'Indeed feminists might well say that Niebuhr has put his finger on what they find to be so worrying about the male world.'[24] Males attempt to be self-sufficient. They attempt to dominate others. But women's sin lies in the way they negate themselves by depending upon others for their self-definition.[25]

Although not writing about Niebuhr's theology as such, Henri Blocher raises important questions about searching for some essence of sin. He helpfully points out that Scripture employs over fifty Hebrew and Greek terms to describe human perversity. The chief amongst these are those words that we translate in English as 'sin' (the idea of missing the mark), 'transgression' (the idea of crossing a moral boundary) and 'iniquity' (a state of moral bentness). He is on firm biblical ground, for these three big ideas are clustered together in significant biblical texts (Exodus 34:6–7; Psalm 51:1–5; Daniel 9:24). Moreover, Blocher argues that only creatures have essences, whereas sin is a corruption. He writes: 'Its [sin's] existence is parasitic; it borrows, or rather usurps, its reality from whatever it corrupts.'[26] Thus, according to Blocher, it is difficult to identify an essence of sin, although many candidates have been suggested historically, including pride, sensuousness, selfishness, unbelief, greed, violence and inertia.[27]

Blocher's warning about the difficulty of identifying the essence of sin is salutary. Instructively, when Paul discusses the sin of Adam in Romans 5 he does not mention pride, but uses a variety of other ideas, which may be translated as in the English Standard Version 'sin' (v. 12), 'transgression' (v. 13), 'trespass' (v. 15) and 'disobedience' (v. 19). In fact, one of the contrasts between Adam and Christ that Paul draws is not one between pride (Adam) and humility (Christ), but the disobedience of Adam as opposed to the obedience of Christ (*parakoē* versus '*upakoē*, Romans 5:19). Indeed, in the Genesis narrative, pride is not obviously the sin of Adam, let alone Eve. Eve is seduced by the serpent's misrepresentation of God. Her attention is drawn to the tree of the knowledge of good and evil. Its fruit seems good to eat, it is a delight to the eyes and can make one wise. As for Adam, all we learn is that he listened to his wife and did what she did (cf. Genesis 3:17). Accordingly, both disobeyed God's command. Arguably, behind the disobedience was not so much pride as unbelief in God's word of command and goodness.

It is also significant, and perhaps a necessary corrective to Niebuhr's account, that Paul *does* allow for certain kinds of pride and boasting. For example, he is prepared to take pride in the cross. He will not boast of himself, but will boast of Christ crucified (*kauchaomai*, Galatians 6:14). He will boast in the Lord (*kauchaomai*, 1 Corinthians 1:31). Moreover, he takes pride in the Corinthians (*kauchēsis*, 2 Corinthians 7:4, 8:24). Having reviewed the sweep of biblical testimony about pride both positive and negative, D. L. Okholm wisely counsels: 'The sin of pride is not to be confused with legitimate self-love that recognises one's rightful place in relation to others and God. Nor is it to be confused with rightful expressions of aggressiveness, assertiveness, initiative, self-confidence or self-esteem, or with taking pleasure in praise.'[28] Not all pride is sin.

Niebuhr appreciated

Niebuhr's legacy with regard to the doctrine of sin is at least four-fold: a doctrine of human nature, realism about human nature, an analysis of pride both individual and collective, and the need for truth about pride to be spoken to power. These raise a series of questions for us.

Doctrine of human nature: Finite yet free. In his doctrine of human nature, Niebuhr drew not only upon the Bible but also upon the writings of the 19th century Danish thinker, Søren

Kierkegaard. For Niebuhr, a human being 'stands at the juncture of nature and spirit; and is involved in both freedom [as spirit] and necessity [as part of nature].'[29]

He sums up the human situation in the following way: 'In short, man, being both free and bound, both limited and limitless, is anxious. Anxiety inevitably accompanies the paradox of freedom and finiteness in which man is involved, and anxiety is the internal precondition of sin.'[30] The idea that anxiety is the precondition to sin, and leaves humanity vulnerable to temptation, is drawn from Kierkegaard. Niebuhr judges that 'Kierkegaard's analysis of the relation of anxiety to sin is the profoundest in Christian thought.'[31]

Although Niebuhr's doctrine of human nature and theology of sin are open to a number of criticisms, he rightly sought to situate his discussion of human sin within the framework of a doctrine of humanity.[32] That is to say, he placed his discussion within a bigger picture. Discussing any of the deadly sins ultimately requires an understanding of what we are truly like outside of Eden, being both finite and fallen. Niebuhr's writings remind us that underlying and informing every ethic is some assumed doctrine of human nature. (This is true even of post-modern theories that argue that there is no such thing as human nature. Human nature is merely a social construct on this view; but ironically, this claim too is a doctrine of human nature.)

Realism, not romanticism. As Colin E. Gunton suggests, 'a number of contemporary theological movements would profit from a careful study of his thought, particularly perhaps his warnings against the romantic elements in some philosophies.'[33] In the light of the Bible's teaching on sin, and the insights of Augustine and Kierkegaard, Niebuhr rejected forms of utopian thinking that are based upon some notion of human perfectibility and upon an unfounded confidence in human progress. Niebuhr thought that democracies especially were tempted to be excessively optimistic at their peril. He had a deep suspicion of utopian illusions.[34] As a result, Niebuhr's theology has been labelled 'Christian Realism'.[35] However, he was no pessimist. His realism attempted a balance between excessive optimism and excessive pessimism. He argued:

A consistent pessimism in regard to man's rational capacity for justice leads to absolutistic political theories; for they prompt the conviction that only preponderant power can coerce the various vitalities of a community into a working harmony. But a too consistent optimism in regard to man's ability to grant justice to his fellows obscures the perils of chaos which perennially confront every society, including a free society.[36]

Pride: Individual and collective.

One of the strengths of Niebuhr's analysis of pride is that he considered not only the individual but also the collective. He observed that an otherwise moral individual may behave far worse in a group than he or she would do if isolated from it.[37] He was particularly critical of the naivety of educators, social scientists and liberal theologians who thought that collectives were simply the individual writ large and that what may work in changing the behaviour of the individual also works for the group.

Niebuhr thought that liberalism, both religious and secular, 'seemed to be unconscious of the basic difference between the morality of individuals and the morality of collectives, whether races, classes or nations'.[38] He believed that there is 'collective egoism' in which 'the egoistic impulses of individuals ... achieve a more vivid expression and cumulative effect when they are united in a common impulse than when they express themselves separately and discreetly.'[39] He argued: 'Our contemporary culture fails to realise the power, extent and persistence of group egoism in human relations.'[40] Hence in his view, group behaviour can breed terrible forms of fanaticism,[41] none more so than the group behaviour of religious people. Militant Islam may illustrate his point in today's world. The will-to-power in the service of pride or the will-to-preserve power to sustain pride are found in churches as well. Both sorts may be seen in the long history of Christianity.

Niebuhr's thesis is a sound one, and his analysis rings true. The 'ethic' of a mob may express itself in brutalities that some individuals within it would otherwise reject in horror. The lynch mob comes to mind, as does the corrupt board of a corporation.

Pride, power and politics. Speaking God's truth to those in power has precedents in both the Old Testament and the New. Elijah confronted King Ahab and Queen Jezebel over the murder of Naboth and the theft, in effect, of his vineyard (1 Kings 21). John the Baptist preached against King Herod's immorality and it cost him his life (Mark 6:14–29). Paul fearlessly preached righteousness, self-control and the coming judgment of God to the Roman governor Felix (Acts 24:24–25).

Niebuhr also spoke truth to power. He believed that an inevitable consequence of the pride of power was injustice. In his view, the prophets of Israel recognised the connection between pride, power and injustice. He wrote: 'Kings and emperors, oligarchs and aristocrats, empires and civilisation all illustrate this perennial sin [injustice] of all men: Seeking [sic.] to transcend the insecurities of finiteness through power, they involve themselves in the insecurities of sin.'[42]

Hence as historian Arthur Schlesinger Jr. says, 'Niebuhr was a critic of national innocence, which he regarded as a delusion.' In particular, he attacked 'the messianic consciousness in the mind of America.'[43] (Interestingly Arthur Schlesinger Jr. is the founder of a group called 'Atheists for Niebuhr', whose existence testifies to Niebuhr's impact well beyond church circles.) On radio Niebuhr said that he believed that a negative part of America's Puritan inheritance was the idea of America having a special destiny by the providence of God.[44] Nations with so much power are tempted to become vain and self-righteous. Niebuhr wrote on one occasion: 'The nation pretends to be God.'[45] For example, Niebuhr contended that a democracy 'cannot of course engage in an explicit preventive war' because of 'the depth of evil to which individuals and communities may sink, particularly when they try to play the role of God in history.'[46] Living as we do post 9/11 and the Twin Towers, these are wise words based on a deep understanding of the flaws in human nature when expressed in the public sphere and in foreign policy.

Questions for us. Niebuhr's analysis of pride arms us with helpful diagnostic questions about the nature of the various 'prides' that we each experience:

Am I experiencing 'the pride of power', where my ego is so secure in my own abilities that I have slipped into thinking that I am much greater than my creaturely limitations? If so, then I may need to remember again the boundaries of my body, the frailty of my human flesh, and the finitude of my life.

Am I experiencing 'the pride of knowledge', where I imagine that the truth as I know it is final and complete for all time? Although Christians understand God to have such knowledge and although we rejoice in whatever he graciously conveys to us, we may yet need to remember that our apprehension of knowledge is incomplete, coloured by our desires and limited by our perspectives. I may need to remember what it is to know truth in humble dependence upon God and in recognition of my propensity to 'spin' the truth in a way that suits me.

Am I experiencing 'the pride of virtue', or moral pride, where I imagine my own standards equal those of God, and where I censure whoever disagrees with me? If so I may need to admit that I have begun to worship and follow myself in reality and Jesus in name only. I may need to recall that whatever has become 'good' in me is only so because of the creative work of

God the Father, the saving work of God the Son, and the regenerating work of God the Holy Spirit.

Christians are often used to interrogating their thoughts and actions as *individuals*; but how do the *groups* we belong to behave? Niebuhr very helpfully draws our attention to the way pride can also be a group sin, and his observations raise some important questions, because this kind of pride can come upon us unexpectedly. If Niebuhr is correct, the behaviour of groups can 'license' us to be proud in ways that we would never accept of ourselves as individuals, and to behave in ways that we would never condone in others.

How do you behave in your various groups? The question is important in relation to whatever secular groups you belong to; but to be more specific, how does your Christian group behave, and how do you behave in it? We must not be naïve. Groups can be the venue for the three kinds of pride that Niebuhr describes.

Although power can be used in the service of Christ and others, the question becomes *how* you and your group use whatever power you might have to further an agenda. Power can be used to exclude and marginalise others, even when no gospel truth is at stake.

So also with knowledge: although it can be used to inform and serve people, the theologically trained can use their knowledge to display their 'superiority' over others rather than to build others up. In doing so, they forget that the secret things still belong to the Lord (Deuteronomy 29:29), that we know only in part (1 Corinthians 13:12), and that knowledge 'puffs up' (1 Corinthians 8:1).

In the realm of morality, careful attention to right and wrong can bring safety, harmony and peace to a group. But a group can become so convinced of its goodness, excellence and holiness that it is no longer open to the reforming word of God. For surely (we reason), my group of 'right-thinking', like-minded' people cannot possibly all be wrong.

Christians can behave badly. Sadly, as church history testifies, Christians in a group can behave even more badly.

Conclusion

There is a temptation born of the Enlightenment of the 18th century to think that humanity has within itself the resources to surmount any difficulty it faces. It is so easy to fall into the Socratic fallacy—that ignorance is the chief problem humanity confronts, and that the key to overcoming it is a good education for all. The Socratic fallacy can be compounded by the addition of the technocratic fallacy, as though education with the addition of correct technique will solve all.

However, Niebuhr draws us back to the Bible and its account of the human predicament, especially of human pride. We live outside of Eden. This is not to say that education and technology are of little or no value. They can be great goods. But who is doing the educating and who is wielding the technology? The biblical answer is: 'Sinners who need a saviour.' Niebuhr was very much aware of this need.

Although Reinhold Niebuhr may have attempted to make the concept of sin as pride do too much explanatory work, his writing helps us to remember that '[t]he cross, which stands at the centre of the Christian worldview, reveals both the seriousness of human sin and the purpose and power of God to overcome it.'[47] Without the grace that is seen in the cross, we overreach ourselves and are undone by our pride. But the cross of Christ, both in what it signifies and in what it achieves, is the antidote to the dark side of pride.

BIOGRAPHY OF REINHOLD NIEBUHR[1]

Although described as 'the supreme American theologian of the 20th century',[2] Reinhold Niebuhr did not see himself as theologian but as someone interested in 'the defence and justification of the Christian faith in a secular age.'[3]

He was born in Wright City, Missouri in 1892, the son of a German Evangelical pastor. Niebuhr studied for the ministry in Eden Theological Seminary and Yale Divinity School, and left Yale established in the theological liberalism of his day.[4] Niebuhr recounted that when his generation graduated from theological seminaries, the credal truths of Christian hope—forgiveness of sins, resurrection of the body, life everlasting—were 'an offence and a stumbling-block to young theologians'.[5]

He witnessed much industrial unrest when serving in a Detroit pastorate during the turbulent years of 1915–1928. He became a social activist and championed organised labour when he saw what Henry Ford's automotive dream actually did to factory workers.[6] 'I cut my eyeteeth fighting Henry Ford,' as he once put it.[7]

Niebuhr left this pastorate in 1928 to join the faculty of New York's Union Theological Seminary, where he became a leading spokesperson for a religious form of socialism.[8] He became disappointed in the fractious and idealistic nature of religious socialism, and began to develop an increasing realism about the flaws in human nature, which was reinforced by the rise of Nazism. Abandoning his pacifism in 1940, his seminal works during the wartime years included keen observations about human failure. For example in 1944 he wrote the oft-quoted aphorism that '[m]an's capacity for justice makes democracy possible; but man's inclination to injustice makes democracy necessary.[9]

During his long career he wrote and spoke on Christianity, politics and social justice, and 'embodied the idea of public theology'.[10] In 1964 he was publicly honoured with the Presidential Freedom Award for Distinguished Service. For Martin Luther King Jr., Niebuhr offers 'a persistent reminder of the reality of sin on every level of humanity's existence ... and the glaring reality of collective evil'.[11]

He also authored a well-known prayer: 'God, give us grace to accept with serenity the things that cannot be changed, courage to change the things that should be changed, and the wisdom to discern the one from the other.' These wise prayers, and his canny observations on human individual and social behaviour, perhaps illustrate the fulfilment of Jesus' promise to send wise men and teachers to his people (Matthew 23:34). Niebuhr died in 1971.

ENDNOTES

1. For a brief but excellent discussion of the seven deadly sins in general and pride (*superbia*) in particular see Richard A. Muller, *Dictionary of Latin and Greek Theological Terms: Drawn Principally from Protestant Scholastic Theology* (Grand Rapids, Michigan: Baker 1986), 280–281.

2. Dante Alighieri, *The Divine Comedy. 2. Purgatory* tr. Dorothy L. Sayers, (Middlesex: Harmondsworth, 1977); cf. 62 and 162.

3. James O. Freedman, 'A Theological Education', *The Chronicle Of Higher Education* 51 no. 43 (2005), B9.

4. Reinhold Niebuhr, 'Intellectual Autobiography', in *Reinhold Niebuhr: His Religious, Social and Political Thought*, eds Charles W. Kegley and Robert W. Bretall (New York: MacMillan, 1961), 6.

5. Ibid. cf. 15 and 9.

6. Reinhold Niebuhr, *The Nature and Destiny of Man: Volume 1, Human Nature* (New York: Charles Scribner; reprinted 1964; originally published 1941), 186, 192 & 213. It is important to note that Niebuhr also considered sensuality a significant dimension of sin, but 'a secondary consequence of man's rebellion against God,' 231. My focus is on his treatment of pride, however. For an analysis of Niebuhr on sin see David L. Smith, *With Wilful Intent: A Theology of Sin* (Wheaton, Illinois: Bridgepoint, 1994), 119–123.

7. Niebuhr, *Nature and Destiny*, 179.

8. Ibid., 180, where Niebuhr quotes from the King James Version.

9. Ibid., 178–183.

10. Ibid., 186–187 n.1. I have followed Niebuhr's own order of names, which is not the chronological order.

11. Ibid., 188.

12. Ibid., 189 n.8. Niebuhr cites Isaiah 47:3–7; Revelation 18:7 and Zephaniah 2:15 as evidence.

13. Ibid., 188–192.

14. Ibid., 195.

15. Ibid., 194–198.

16. Ibid., 199.

17. Ibid., 200.

18. Ibid., 208.

19. Ibid., 213.

20. Ibid., 214. Niebuhr cites Isaiah 47; Jeremiah 25:15 and Ezekiel 24–39 as evidence.

21. Ibid., 219.

22. William John Wolf, 'Reinhold Niebuhr's Doctrine Of Man', in *Reinhold Niebuhr: His Religious, Social and Political Thought*, eds Charles W. Kegley and Robert W. Bretall, (New York: MacMillan 1961), 241.

23. Ibid., 240–241.

24. Quoted in Alister E. McGrath, *The Christian Theology Reader* Third Edition, (Malden, MA: Blackwell, 2007), 480.

25. Ibid., 482. Hampson draws on the work of Valerie Saiving and Judith Plaskow especially in her critique.

26. I am indebted for the substance of this paragraph to H. G. A. Blocher, 'Sin', in *New Dictionary Of Biblical Theology*, eds T. D. Alexander and Brian S Rosner, (Leicester: IVP, 2000). For a similar point about the essence of sin, see R. R. Reno, 'Sin, Doctrine of', in *Dictionary for the Theological Interpretation of the Bible*, ed. Kevin J. Vanhoozer, (London/Grand Rapids, MI: SPCK/ Baker, 2006).

27. Blocher, 'Sin', 783.

28. D. L. Okholm, 'Pride', in *New Dictionary Of Christian Ethics And Pastoral Theology*, eds David J. Atkinson and David H. Field, (Leicester/Downers Grove: Inter-Varsity, 1995).

29. Niebuhr, *Nature and Destiny*, 181.

30. Ibid., 182.

31. Ibid. n.2.

32. For more criticisms as well as an appreciation see Colin E. Gunton, *Theology Through The Theologians* (Edinburgh: T. & T. Clark, 1996), 218–220.

33. Ibid., 206.

34. Dennis P. McCann, *Christian Realism and Liberation Theology; Pracitcal Theologies in Creative Conflict*, (Maryknoll N.Y.: Orbis, 1981), 128.

35. 'Christian realism' is an expression that Niebuhr used himself. See Niebuhr, 'Autobiography', 10.

36. Reinhold Niebuhr, *The Children of Light and the Children of Darkness* (New York: Charles Scribner; reprinted 1972; originally published 1944), xii.

37. Since Niebuhr wrote, famous investigations made by psychologists such as Samuel Ash and Stanley Milgram seem strongly to support Niebuhr's view. For a useful entrée into this and other such research, see Richard Swedberg, 'Civil courage (*Zivilcourage*): The case of Knut Wicksell', *Theory and Society* 28 no. 4 (1999), 526 n.46. I owe this helpful reference to Andrew Cameron and am in his debt for numerous helpful suggestions now incorporated into this chapter.

38. Reinhold Niebuhr, *Moral Man and Immoral Society* (New York: Charles Scribner; reprinted 1960; originally published 1932), ix. Twenty-eight years after its first publication, in 1960 Niebuhr endorsed this observation as still his view.

39. Ibid., xii.

40. Ibid., xxii.

41. Ibid., 277.

42. Reinhold Niebuhr, *Beyond Tragedy: Essays on the Christian Intrepretation of History (New York: Charles Scribner; reprinted 1965; originally published 1937)*, 102–103.

43. Arthur Schlesinger Jr., 'Forgetting Reinhold Niebuhr', *New York Times*, 18th September 2005. n.p.

44. Niebuhr, quoted by Krista Tippett, 'Moral Man And Immoral Society: The Public Theology of Reinhold Niebuhr', in *Speaking of Faith* (American Public Media, 2006); online: http://speakingoffaith.publicradio.org/programs/neibuhr/transcript.shtml. n.p.

45. Niebuhr, *Nature and Destiny*, 212.

46. Schlesinger Jr., 'Forgetting Reinhold Niebuhr', n.p.

47. Niebuhr, *Beyond Tragedy*, x.

BIOGRAPHICAL ENDNOTES

1. For a brief but useful introduction to Reinhold Niebuhr see Roger L. Shinn, 'Niebuhr, Reinhold and H. Richard', in *The Oxford Companion To Christian Thought: Intellectual, Spiritual, and Moral Horizons of Christianity*, ed. Adrian Hastings, (Oxford: Oxford University Press, 2000). Reinhold's brother, H. Richard Niebuhr was also a major theologian.

2. Arthur Schlesinger Jr., 'Forgetting Reinhold Niebuhr', *New York Times*, 18th September 2005, 6; online: http://www.nytimes.com/2005/09/18/books/review/18schlesinger.html?ex=1169787600&en=60f51bda8f871895&ei=5070 (accessed 24/1/2007).

3. Reinhold Niebuhr, 'Intellectual Autobiography', in *Reinhold Niebuhr: His Religious, Social and Political Thought*, eds Charles W. Kegley and Robert W. Bretall, (New York: MacMillan, 1961), 3.

4. Dennis P. McCann, *Christian Realism And Liberation Theology: Practical Theologies In Creative Conflict* (Maryknoll N.Y.: Orbis, 1981), 8.

5. Reinhold Niebuhr, *Beyond Tragedy: Essays on the Christian Interpretation of History* (New York: Charles Scribner; reprinted 1965; originally published 1937), 288–289.

6. McCann, *Christian Realism*, 9.

7. Niebuhr, quoted by Krista Tippett, 'Moral Man And Immoral Society: The Public Theology Of Reinhold Niebuhr', in *Speaking of Faith* (American Public Media, 2006); online: http://speakingoffaith.publicradio.org/programs/niebuhr/transcript.shtml.

8. McCann, *Christian Realism*, 10.

9. Reinhold Niebuhr, *The Children of Light and the Children of Darkness* (New York: Charles Scribner; reprinted 1972; originally published 1944), xiii.

10. Tippett, 'Moral Man', n.p.

11. Quoted in Warren Goldstein, 'A Liberal Dose of Religious Fervor', *The Chronicle Of Higher Education* 51 no. 44 (2005), B6.

CALVIN ON SLOTH
PETER JENSEN

In the modern mind, the word 'sloth' is more likely to conjure up images of a mammal hanging from a tree in Central America than a fatal weakness of character. Earlier generations of Christians, especially those of the medieval period, paid a great deal of attention to sloth. This is reflected in their vocabulary for analysing the sin: laziness, carelessness, tardiness, listlessness, indolence, torpor, sluggishness, languor, weariness, dullness, and coldness. It is true that most parents object to laziness in their teenage children, and the average taxpayer resents 'dole bludgers'. However, in the Christian circles in which I move the sin is rarely attacked. What have we been missing? Would consideration of human sloth add something important to our proclamation of the gospel and the edification of Christ's people?

The sluggard: something to offer?

To take one prime example, it has become the custom among my contemporaries to speak of the fundamental sin as 'rebellion against God'. So habitual has such language become that it is hard to think in any other terms and hard to recognise that this does not exhaust the biblical categories. To speak of rebellion is not wrong in itself; it has the great advantage of reminding us what lies at the heart of human pride, and what must therefore lie at the heart of human repentance. It is not wrong, but is it adequate?

Rebellion is active. Mutineers are those who take up arms against lawful authority and overthrow it. The idea of spiritual sloth or sluggishness opens up a new perspective that surely corresponds to other aspects of human experience in a profound way. One of the most memorable of biblical characters is the sluggard in Proverbs 6:9–11. He has trouble turning over in bed, putting food into his mouth, tending his crops or in any way looking after his own interests, let alone the interests of others. He is helpless and useless and as his laziness becomes compounded, so his position worsens as the days pass. To use the language of rebellion exclusively is to miss this element of experience and to leave the problems of human existence partially undiagnosed.

Better to be a bludger or a workaholic?

There is a related contemporary issue that cannot be ignored in a study of this kind. As those who live in the era of the global economy, we are increasingly aware of the demands being made on our lives by work. A recent study, *An Unexpected Tragedy,* has drawn attention to the significant impact of changing work patterns on the quality of family life, friendships, and community involvement. On average, we are working longer hours, more weekends and weeknights, and more often on a casual basis, than our parents. And our children are suffering for it. The consequences can be measured in terms of 'negative health outcomes', 'strained family relationships', and 'parenting marked by anger, inconsistency, and ineffectiveness'.[1] The need to purchase a house, when the cost of housing has become prohibitive, means long hours of extra effort. The work place advantages won by the trade unions in earlier generations are being lost. The shared weekend is at risk. In the capitalist system, sloth is not an option: it is a leading sin. Is not our busyness a greater fault than sloth? Is our problem the opposite of sloth?

It is interesting to note that the list of seven deadly (or 'capital') sins is not strictly biblical. Thus, for example, sloth is not condemned in the Decalogue or the Sermon on the Mount and nor is it one of the sins of the flesh mentioned in Mark 7 or Galatians 5. In a word-study of the New Testament, the word hardly appears at all, and when it does, as in Romans 12:11, 'never be lacking in zeal, but keep your spiritual fervour, serving the Lord', it seems incidental to the main point, which is enthusiasm in the Lord's service. There is also a different word (lazy, sluggish) in Hebrews 6:12, 'We do not want you to become lazy...' where the chief point is diligence (6:11). Naturally, the concept may be found elsewhere, such as in the description of the Laodicean church in Revelation 3:15, 'neither cold nor hot'. Is the sin of sloth less culpable than it seemed to earlier generations?

Help from Calvin

Before we dismiss criticism of sloth as an unhealthy preoccupation of medieval theologians we will do well to turn to John Calvin for guidance. To some, the choice of Calvin will seem perverse. Is not Calvinism itself largely responsible for the 'Protestant work ethic' and its erosion of time for family and leisure in the name of industry? Under the impact of the Reformation, work of all sorts was dignified as a calling. Hard work was honoured, as 'unto the Lord'. Calvin frequently condemned laziness. Success that accompanied hard work done in the right way bred a spirit of success. R. H. Tawney famously argued that for later generations of Calvinists (notably the English Puritans), success in business was equated with the blessing of God and served to reinforce assurance of salvation itself. At the same time the ancient condemnation of usury was weakened, and the way opened for the development to the capitalist economy. Does Calvin's emphasis actually help facilitate an unhealthy spiritual and physical lifestyle? Is there something to be said in favour of sloth?

For a range of reasons that will become obvious, I am convinced Calvin has much to offer on this subject. I am a great admirer of John Calvin, although I am not a Calvin scholar. Given that sloth is not a category we are accustomed to use when we discuss the spiritual life, Calvin's frequent references to sloth and its allies is a challenge to us. Perhaps Calvin offers us at this point a helpful corrective—more, a tool to diagnose the spiritual condition of humanity.

BIOGRAPHY OF JOHN CALVIN

The reformer John Calvin was born at Noyon, France in 1509. Calvin's father first intended him for the church and so he went to Paris in 1523 to study theology. However, his father redirected John's career path in 1528 and he moved to Orleans to study law. With his father's death in 1531, Calvin supplemented his study of law with Hebrew and classical subjects. In 1532 he had what he later described as his 'conversion' which he attributed to the mercy and grace of God: 'Since I was too obstinately devoted to the superstitions of popery to be easily extricated from so profound an abyss of mire, God, by sudden conversion, subdued and brought my mind to a teachable frame.' His association with Nicholas Cop, the Rector of the University of Paris, caused Calvin to flee the French capital in 1533 when Cop provoked Catholic fury by giving an address that was decidedly Protestant. During 1535–6 Calvin exiled himself to Basle where he devoted his time to writing a textbook of the reformed faith. This was the first edition of his celebrated **Institutes of the Christian Religion**. Four later editions culminated in the 1559 version of the work, which has come to be accepted as Calvin's theological masterpiece. In 1536 he began his long association with the city of Geneva. Although Calvin only planned to stay overnight in Geneva, William Farel convinced him to remain and assist with further reformation of the church in that city. Apart from a three-year exile beginning in 1538 when Calvin and Farel were expelled by the city council because it was felt their reforms were too drastic, he remained the city's chief pastor for the rest of his life, dying in 1564.

Few theologians have had more influence on Protestant thinking than John Calvin. His teaching spread all over Europe and became the doctrinal basis of Presbyterianism and other reformed churches. He was an incredibly prolific writer, producing the *Institutes*, as well as many biblical commentaries and other works.[2] Calvin kept himself busy for he knew that one of 'the effects of sin' was that it makes human beings 'slothful when they should be diligent'. Yet sloth was not only a problem for the unregenerate, it remained a temptation for the redeemed.

Sloth and the work place

The proverbs that condemn the indolence of the sluggard, commend instead the industry of a tiny insect:

> Go to the ant, you sluggard; consider its ways and be wise!
> It has no commander, no overseer or ruler, yet it stores its
> provisions in summer and gathers its food at harvest
> (Proverbs 6:6–8).

This is just one small contribution to the Bible's teaching about work. The biblical doctrine of work is a complex and lengthy study. But it is clear that work is part of the very purpose of human life; that since the fall human labour has been difficult and sometimes unrewarding; that our everyday work is part of our worship, part of the 'works' we do to the glory of God; there is honour, but no special glory, in being set apart for religious 'work'; that we are to work with all our might even for the unresponsive or unjust employer; that employers must be just; that we, and those who work for us, are to rest from our work on a weekly basis. On all these things we may expect to find Calvin in substantial agreement.

On the other hand, Calvin has an emphasis which goes slightly further. In talking of the appointment of the Sabbath, Calvin makes the point that God's rest does not indicate that he has ceased from work, since he still upholds all things. Rather, the seventh day was appointed for meditation on the works and ways of God: 'God claims for himself the meditations and employments of men on the seventh day.' He continues, 'The design of the institution must be always kept in memory: for God did not command men simply to keep holiday every seventh day, as if he delighted in their indolence; but rather that they, being released from all other business, might more readily apply their minds to the Creator of the world' (on Genesis 2:3). Likewise, although the psalmist tells us that sleep is a gift from the Lord to his servants, Calvin spiritualises: 'as we know that men are created with the design of their being occupied (in work) ... it is certain that the word *sleep* is not to be understood as implying slothfulness, but a placid labour'. This he defines as the repose of the mind by faith in the midst of busyness, 'as if they were asleep' (on Psalm 127:2). The Christian life of 'placid labour' has little room for holiday, for pastimes, for what we may call recreation. In his comment on the fourth commandment (Exodus 20:8) Calvin says:

> Surely God has no delight in idleness and sloth, and therefore there was no importance in the simple cessation of the labours of their hands and feet; nay, it would have been a childish superstition to rest with no other view than to occupy their repose in the service of God.

Elsewhere he adds, 'It is certain that indolence and idleness are accursed by God. Besides, we know that man was created with this view, that he might do something' (on 2 Thessalonians 3:10). There is an intensity here, as elsewhere in Calvin, which lays upon the human spirit a response to God of an all-consuming nature. Personally, I find it less than attractive—all the more reason for me to be challenged and to ask myself whether I am not too much a practitioner of the sin of sloth.

Sloth as a disease of the spirit

Calvin's real interest is not in the sort of sloth that is displayed by the sluggard, a work-shy lazy person. Naturally, as we have seen he would oppose such a life-style consistently. Indeed he is particularly harsh on those in positions of responsibility, such as pastors and princes who go about their labours in a slipshod, careless manner. But his references to sloth are to a more serious fault than mere laziness. For Calvin, an immensely busy person may still be slothful where it really counts, namely in the affairs of the Spirit, in the response to God. Indeed, when it comes to the things of God, he sees us all as naturally sluggish and indifferent. Here lies the real peril of sloth, not in the sluggard refusing to work, but in the spiritual lassitude of even the busy person when it comes to matters of eternal significance. We may have some hint of what he is speaking about if we reflect on the analogy of our natural reluctance to break bad eating habits and to engage in exercise, even though we know that such disciplined behaviour is strongly in our best interests. We prefer to fill our days with a multitude of less important things.

Calvin sees this failing in Lot. Placed in a perilous situation, and in need of immediate action to save himself and his family, Lot hesitates. Although he believes the word by which God has warned him of judgment:

> As if sinking under his own infirmity, and entangled with many cares, he, who ought to have run forth hastily and without delay, moves with slow and halting pace. In his person, however, the Spirit of God presents to us, as in a mirror, our own tardiness, in order that we, shaking off all sloth, may learn to prepare ourselves for prompt obedience, as soon as the heavenly voice sounds in our ears; otherwise, in addition to that indolence which, by nature, dwells within us, Satan will interpose many delays (on Genesis 19:15).

Here is an analysis of the human situation that matches experience. There is a natural unwillingness to attend to God and his word, a certain drowsiness of the soul. But this natural sloth is increased by everyday life, the pressures of time and relationships that distract us from what matters. Calvin also reminds us that the devil will exploit the situation and discourage our desire to obey God, even when we believe that God has addressed us. Like Jesus in the parable of the sower, however, Calvin recognises that whereas the anxieties and cares of life may encourage our natural spiritual torpor, so too may luxury and ease:

The corruption and depravity of human nature make it scarcely possible for the world to enjoy ease and prosperity without becoming indolent. Next, falling gradually into slothfulness, it will deceive itself by a false imagination, and drive away from it all fear, and relying on this confidence, will insolently rise up against God (on Isaiah 32:9–10).

The last quotation reminds us that there is no sharp division between sloth and rebellion. Our indifference to God is a result of sin and it is the ground of our active sins against the majesty of God and his word. We cannot hide behind sloth or excuse ourselves as though it is merely natural and not vicious. Passivity in the presence of God's word is rebellion. Thus Calvin's emphasis on the sin of sloth does not contradict the concept of sin as rebellion; it adds depth to it as we see that rebellion comes in different forms and arises from different sources. The category of sloth enables Calvin to add a moral and culpable significance to the ignorance of God, as he says:

The eyes of men are darkened by slothfulness, because they neither inquire, nor consider, nor observe. Thus they are stupefied by idols, for they are willingly deceived ... This shows that idolaters cannot be excused on the pleas of ignorance, for they choose to be blind and to wander in darkness (on Isaiah 41:28).

Justifying sloth because God is sovereign

Calvin is keenly aware that Christians may use the doctrine of God's sovereignty as an excuse for idleness: 'it is a perversion to make the providence of God an excuse for negligence and sloth' (on Exodus 2:1). One of the great strengths of his theology is the way in which he allows the biblical word on the sovereignty of God its full say. The biblical account leaves no room for a God who works with the world as an equal partner, while he waits upon the wills of human beings to make decisions of which he may or may not approve. He is, to quote Paul, the one who 'works out everything in conformity with the purpose of his will' (Ephesians 1:11). But does this leave room for human effort and energy?

The paradox is that not only does the biblical doctrine leave room for human effort—it actually encourages strenuous effort. There is a telling commentary by Calvin on Joshua, after that warrior had received a promise of victory as recorded in Joshua 10:8. It may be imagined that such a promise may have absolved Joshua from any need to exert himself in battle. Calvin, without doubt, understands the biblical view better than that:

> It is moreover worthy of notice that Joshua did not abuse the divine promise by making it an excuse for sluggishness, but felt the more vehemently inflamed after he was assured of a happy issue. Many, while they ostentatiously express their faith, become lazy and slothful from perverse security. Joshua hears that victory is in his hand, and that he may gain it, runs swiftly into battle. For he knew that the happy issue was revealed, not for the purpose of slackening his pace or making him more remiss, but of making him exert himself with greater zeal.

At the back of the paradox lies the biblical understanding of creation. On the one hand the Bible presents us with a picture of God as sovereign over all things in creation, counting the very hairs on our head and marking the fall of the sparrow. It is very clear that he does not need us to accomplish his will and purpose in the world. He can and does act directly. And yet it is also clear that he delights to act indirectly, or, as the older theologians used to say, through secondary causes. He is pleased to use the activities of the animal kingdom to sustain the world, for example, allowing what we would call the natural course of things to produce what he could produce instantaneously if he should so wish.

The world is utterly dependent on God from moment to moment. But he has incorporated into creation an indirect way of doing things that enables his creatures, and especially his human and angelic creatures, to enjoy a 'dependent independence'. That is, he weaves our free activities into his purposes, never frustrated even by sin. We see this in prayer. God clearly does not need the prayers of his people in order to act, and yet he calls on us to pray and assures us that our prayers have real effects. He incorporates our prayers as instruments by which he rules the world, neither abandoning his sovereignty nor nullifying human effort. Paul expresses this in Philippians 2:12,13: 'continue to work out your salvation with fear and trembling, for it is God who works in you to will and to act according to his good purpose.'

Referring to this passage, Calvin observes:

(Paul) ascribes to them a part in acting that they may not engage in carnal sloth, but by enjoining fear and trembling, he humbles them so as to keep them in remembrance, that the very thing which they are ordered to do is the proper work of God—distinctly intimating, that believers act (if I may so speak) *passively* in as much as the power is given to them from heaven, and cannot in any way be arrogated to themselves (*Institutes* 2.5.11).

In short, God does not need us, but he sees fit, graciously, to use us. For us to defy him by sloth will not frustrate his plans and purposes, but it will deprive us of the honour and joy of working with him in his appointed way. For us, like Joshua, to regard the promise of the Lord as an invitation to seek the blessing of God by participating with him in his work is a path of natural Christian godliness. The knowledge of the sovereignty of God does not create passivity—it energises and encourages us to zeal and enthusiasm, knowing that we are participating with God in his work through us.

Combating the slothful spirit

Already we have begun to see what Calvin has to teach us about how to overcome spiritual sloth. Of course the greatest victory over spiritual lassitude is when by God's word and Spirit we come to know God, we come alive to God. But in Calvin's account of the Christian life, we continue to wage fierce warfare against sin, the world and the devil, until our life's end. This is a stern and unremitting conflict although not without the help of God and its own progress. At every point, however, the pattern is the same, namely, that we are to struggle with all our might and we are to do so only in the strength that God provides and with thankfulness to him. The struggle does not belong partly to God and partly to us, but wholly to God and wholly to us. When it comes to sloth in particular the keenest battle is to do with obedience to God's word. Will we obey God or not?

If we consider our own part in this combat, each of us is to 'reprove his own slothfulness'. When we fail to praise God as we should, the remedy is that 'every man may descend into himself and correct his own sluggishness' (on Psalm 103:1). In broader terms, Calvin calls us to ceaseless mortification, ceaseless scrutiny and correction, and constant repentance. It is a summons that our modern piety hardly reflects at all. We sometimes talk about 'becoming more like Jesus', but the seriousness required for such a project is lacking (2 Peter 1:5–9). Our unwillingness to measure our lives by the full rigour of the law as revealed in the whole of scripture means that we are less and less conscious of our sin, since we have abandoned the God-given means of identifying sin and so forsaking it. At this point, it may be helpful to consider the root causes of our indiscipline and waywardness. How do we correct our sluggishness?

Perhaps, to turn to the other side of the paradox of our relationship with God, it is by casting ourselves on him that our efforts will bear fruit. The sovereign God is also our Father; his project is indeed to 'bring many sons to glory'. Part of his method in doing this is to bring into our lives those disciplines and troubles he sees will be good for us in making us into the image of his Son. There is a path of suffering which he walked and from which no Christian is exempt. For those who have no knowledge of God, such troubles may be very destructive. For those who are trusting God, the same troubles, rightly received, will work good. Calvin regards 'even the best of men' as 'slow and slothful' and so, 'it becomes necessary to chastise them with rods, otherwise they would never approach God of their own accord' (on Daniel 5:6). When we receive the troubles of life appropriately, not in a cowardly way but with confidence that God is our loving and almighty Father, we can make progress in subduing the flesh and withstanding the world and the devil.

Fundamentally, however, the Christian is armed for combat through the word of God, the Spirit of God, prayer, and Christian fellowship. As far as the word is concerned, Calvin sees both the law and the promises of God as integral to the discipline that will help deal with the sloth that so easily afflicts us. It is worth hearing and thinking about Calvin's teaching on the matter:

> The Law acts as a whip to the flesh, urging it on as men
> do a lazy sluggish ass. Even in the case of a spiritual man,
> inasmuch as he is still burdened with the weight of the flesh,
> the Law is a constant stimulus pricking him forward when he
> would indulge in sloth (Institutes 2.7.12).

It is important to note in this context that Calvin rightly links Law and Spirit together. The promise of the New Covenant was that the Law would be written on the heart. The believer turns to Christ because of the powerful work of the Spirit, and, in his or her turn to Christ the Spirit of God 'already flourishes and reigns' in the heart (Institutes 2.7.12). There is no suggestion here that believers are left to struggle on their own.

Of course the word ministers to us in many ways. As well as the Law itself we have the admonitions and exhortations of Scripture and, sometimes even more powerfully, the examples of stories in Scripture for us to meditate and learn from. Likewise there are the mighty works of God in creation and redemption to stimulate our faith and obedience. As Calvin says:

> It is our duty to rise higher, and to contemplate the invaluable treasures of the kingdom of heaven which he has unfolded in Christ, and all the gifts which belong to the spiritual life, that by reflecting upon these our hearts may be inflamed with love to God, that we may be stirred up to the practice of godliness, and that we may not suffer ourselves to become slothful and remiss in celebrating his praises (on Psalm 8:7–9).

The experience of living for God and before God is often distilled in the scriptures and likewise provides a stimulus for faith and obedience. Thus Calvin notes for example that under the Old Covenant, God's people sometimes made vows to God to help them master their natural sloth. He does not insist on it as a habit, but he allows that it may still be useful to some in some circumstances, especially in dealing with a problem not sinful in itself but undesirable: 'should one be oblivious or sluggish in the necessary duties of piety, why should he not, by forming a vow, both awaken his memory and shake off his sloth?' (*Institutes* 4.13.5).

The other way in which the word ministers to us is through its promises. There are of course, promises of judgment and rebuke, and these should make us fear God and wish all the more fervently to obey him. Nor are such promises directed only at the unbeliever. Believers will stand before the judgment seat of Christ, not to be sure as a matter of eternal salvation but as what may be called stewardship and accountability. Our complacency and sluggishness should be checked and corrected by this consideration. It is true that God is the loving Father but, as Hebrews 12 reminds us, he will still chastise his children.

There are also the promises of reward and mercy to stimulate obedience and fervour. Calvin is at pains to point out how this differs from any hint of salvation by works. The rewards we receive are all premised on the covenant of grace which precedes them; they arise out of the pure mercy of God and not because we deserve to be rewarded. Furthermore, when we obey God, we are simply doing our duty, which gives no ground for a reward. But God treats us kindly, gently and lovingly, rewarding us even though we do not strictly deserve such a gift. God is under no obligation to reward us, but his promise of reward and blessing create in us a desire to please him and walk in his ways.

One way in which God's promises are declared and received is through what Calvin calls 'external helps'; the church, the ministry and the sacraments. Thus, for example, Calvin was strongly of a mind that the Lord's Supper should be a weekly feast for believers, declaring that the practice of yearly communions 'makes the whole year one of sloth'. 'It ought,' he observes, 'to have been far otherwise. Each week, at least, the table of the Lord ought to have been spread for the company of Christians, and the promises declared on which we might then spiritually feed' (*Institutes* 4.17.46). In a contemporary ethos in which the Communion is undervalued in some quarters, here is a challenge from a source whom none can suspect of catholicising tendencies. Is our neglect of the Lord's Supper a sign of spiritual drowsiness? Would we be spiritually stronger by the discipline of frequent communion?

Our prayers are based on God's promises and are a part of our obedience to God. We ought to be frequent and fervent in prayer. But if sloth is to hinder any part of our Christian lives, it will attack at this point. Like the disciples in Gethsemane, our spirits flag and we sleep at our post. To combat this, Calvin would say that as well as attending carefully to the word of promise and admonition, we are to 'long for the aid of the Spirit'. But the aid of the Spirit is no substitute for our own strenuous discipline, since, 'while the inspiration of the Spirit is effectual to the formation of prayer, it by no means impedes or retards our own endeavours; since in this matter God is pleased to try how efficiently faith influences our hearts' (*Institutes* 3.20.5).

The two faces of sloth: idle at worship and work as idol

The two questions with which I began are these. First, has Calvin's testimony to sloth added an important element to our consideration of the spiritual life whether of believers or unbelievers? Calvin wanted to make sloth much more than mere laziness in everyday life. Furthermore, we have also noted that the Scriptures target sloth infrequently.

I have difficulty in resolving the issues raised by this observation. At the level of experience, it seems to me that Calvin has put his finger on something that is unmistakeably true. If we measure our lives beside the commandment to love God with all our heart, soul, strength and mind, we fail dismally. Most of us are troubled by the lack of fervour we feel in the things of God. Most of us are troubled by the sluggishness of our prayer-lives and the distaste we experience from time to time for Christian fellowship or for listening to God's word. To have this problem identified as the sin of sloth is to be given an explanation and an enemy, both very helpful. It certainly deepens our appreciation of the sin of rebellion to which we usually refer.

But I wonder, too, whether we are sometimes identifying sloth with mere creatureliness. Calvin's treatment of sleep— spiritualising Psalm 127:2 'for he grants sleep to those he loves', is suggestive. The gift of sleep he reads as a 'placid labour', as faith. However we may also think of sleep as that which reminds us that we do not rule the world. God does not sleep; he does not need to. But we are mere creatures. We must sleep, and while we do the world continues. The only 'Christian' way to sleep is to sleep as a creature, trusting God. In sleep, we are permitted to forget him. Perhaps the sin would be to reject our role as creatures. And this too is relevant to our second question. Sleep and the Sabbath are gifts from God and a constant reminder that we are creatures. The modern world—and much of the modern ecclesiastical world—want us to believe that we are as indispensable as God himself, who neither slumbers nor sleeps. Our constant busyness creates an affront to our relationships, with God and with others. That the so-called 'protestant work ethic' reflected something of the biblical imperative to work 'as unto the Lord' and thus with all our might, I do not doubt. But it was never an absolute, for then work becomes an idol, and the fruit of our work in the accumulation of mammon becomes even more idolatrous. The Bible tells us both to work and to cease from work. In sleep we rest. The Sabbath enables us to look after our neighbours and to attend to our fellowship with God. The work practices of the modern world are in grave danger of consuming us. They are feeding the sloth towards God that is part of our rebellion against him—our capacity to ignore him by filling our lives with substitutes. Against this John Calvin bears witness with a prophetic voice. We would do well to learn from him.[3]

ENDNOTES

1. Relationships Forum Australia, *An Unexpected Tragedy: Evidence for the connection between working hours and family breakdown in Australia*, 2007, Executive Summary, 14. www.relationshipsforum.org.au/report

2. Quotes from Calvin's commentaries in this chapter simply refer to the relevant Bible text (e.g. 'on Genesis 19.15'). It is not always obvious how the Bible verse relates to Calvin's argument, as he sometimes takes the opportunity to discourse on loosely related ideas. See www.ccel.org/ccel/calvin. [Eds].

3. I am very grateful to Mr Eric Cheung for his assistance in research for this chapter.

STILL DEADLY

SEVEN DEADLY SINS:
AN AFTERWORD

Michael Hill taught at Moore Theological College, the training college for the Diocese of Sydney,[1] as its senior ethicist during two appointments totalling twenty-seven years and spanning 1976 to 2006. This book has been written in his honour, and this afterword is intended to show a little of what he taught and the way our book differs from his approach.

Hill sought for a more rigorously theological account of ethics, and arrived at what (for his students) is the now famous 'mutual love' dictum: 'an action or trait of character is right if and only if it promotes (creates or maintains) mutual love relationships between (a) God and humans, and, (b) humans and humans.'[2] To arrive at this conclusion, he drew upon the character of God revealed in the overall sweep of the biblical story.

His contribution to the rehabilitation of serious reflection in Australian evangelical theological ethics has been very great. He has released several generations of theological students from 'divine command theory deontology', where God commands practices that are required of us solely due to the power of his will, and not necessarily with any connection between the practices and the structures of God's world.

Hill showed how love is grounded in the good structures of God's world.[3] Divine command theory deontology forgets the way God founded his world in wisdom (Proverbs 8), so that God's commands direct our behaviour partly by unveiling the true structure of his world. The good that God commands derives from humanity's nature and purpose, and to love one another is to do this good to one another. Hence 'love' and 'the good' make sense because of the divinely structured purposes of the creation.

In this way Hill frees us to see that the *goal* of God's command is *relationships characterised by love*. This insight is illustrated in the apostle Paul's intriguing comment to Philemon (vv8–9) that although Paul was certainly 'bold enough in Christ to command [Philemon] to do what is required', he appeals instead 'for love's sake'. Even if Paul *had* given a command, it would ultimately have made sense because it promoted love.

So Hill's ethic is *not* interested in reducing ethics just to its virtues, its rules or the results of its actions. For Hill, we are creatures of God built for a community of mutual love, and whatever rules, principles, goals and virtues we find in the Bible spring from this purpose.

But in complete contrast to Hill's method, the 'seven deadly sins' are the flipside of a medieval philosophical theology that summarised 'the good life' as four cardinal and three theological virtues: prudence, justice, temperance, fortitude; and faith, hope and love. However medieval thinkers did *not* consider that each deadly sin was the dark side of each of these virtues. For Thomas Aquinas, 'there is no need for the principal vices to be contrary to the principal virtues'.[4] The virtues arise when we understand whatever goods will not change. But as 1 John 2:17 says, vices arise when we are overcome by goods that change and are passing: 'vice arises from the appetite for mutable good'.[5]

Michael Hill's 'mutual love' dictum is an evangelical Protestant response to the Kantian ethics of the Enlightenment, not an exercise in medieval Catholicism; and his biblical theological approach results in a very different kind of summary of 'the good life' than do the 'seven deadly sins'. So great are these differences that we might appear seriously to dishonour Hill by focussing upon the 'seven deadly sins' in his honour!

Perhaps the reasons given in the preface to the book offer some clues about our odd choice of method. The mode of analytical analysis required by Hill's work is where it remains daunting for some. Not all people can use his tools to imagine the properly loving act, because a particular kind of mental effort is required to generate and apply his mutual love dictum to the practices of life.

Attention to the seven deadly sins has been a teaching tool to enable people to begin to see what love *doesn't*, and hence *does*, look like in several of the small moments of their lives. By arguing against various vices, we have commended other virtues. But the language of virtue ethics, which is amply attested in the New Testament,[6] is a help to us precisely because it offers *brief* descriptions of the way an agent (and his or her affections) intersects with the order of reality that surrounds her, voiced in a supple, varied and creative language. In the heated moment of decision, virtue language offers a statement of *aim*: I can quickly weigh up *who* I want to be in the moment, even if I might need Hill's act analysis and its reflection upon human nature and purpose for less hurried times of reflection and deliberation.

Therefore the subjects of this book should not be taken to represent an exhaustive Christian treatment of how to live. They are only small vignettes in the story of mutual love.

It is tempting to joke about Hill's penchant for illustrating his ethic with slightly oddball references to sex. His days as a young single male teacher, surrounded by slightly clad New Guinean women, keep emerging in his teaching as a series of flashbacks not unlike those of a Vietnam veteran, but with a different set of youthful traumas. Hill's openness about sexuality is uncharacteristic of his generation, and has been of enormous benefit in permitting his generally conservative students to work through their theological ethic of sex. For Hill, marital sexual expression is a mutual self-giving for the good of the other, a bodily expression perfectly suited to its context of faithful lifelong and exclusive mutual grace and love. His delightful appreciation of his married life, first with Christine Thew and then after Christine's untimely death, with Wendy Dahl from 1993, lends these reflections a deeply appealing gravitas. His occasional reflections on the loss of Christine also grace us with an openness and vulnerability that we have never earnt or deserved, yet which reveal to us with unbearable poignancy the honour due to a loving and faithful marriage, the terrible disfigurement that death brings to relationships of mutual love in this fallen world, and yet the prevailing goodness of God, this time in his gift to Michael and Wendy of each other.

Those of us who have benefited most from Hill's work also know that his way of talking about love is an articulation of what we have directly *observed*: his usually gentle, occasionally fierce, and always faithful way with others. Our initiation into 'the how and why of love' has been (in the metaphor of Stanley Hauerwas) an apprenticeship to a master craftsman.

Michael already knows much of the theology profiled here, but we think he will enjoy being further sharpened and stretched by it. May it help Michael, ourselves, and all our readers toward our best and truest desire: a community of mutual love relationships in Christ that 'will find its perfection and completion in the presence of God'.[7]

Andrew Cameron

ENDNOTES

1. Online: http://www.moore.edu.au.
2. Michael Hill, *The How and Why of Love: An Introduction to Evangelical Ethics* (Kingsford: Matthias Media, 2002), 131.
3. Hill borrows here from Oliver M.T. O'Donovan, *Resurrection and Moral Order: An Outline for Evangelical Ethics* (Leicester: Apollos, 1994).
4. Thomas Aquinas, *Summa Theologica* tr. Fathers of the English Dominican Province, (London: Benzinger Brothers, 1937), 1a2ae, q. 84, art. 4, ad. 1.
5. Ibid.
6. Burton Easton found eleven 'virtue-catalogues' and seventeen 'vice-catalogues' in the New Testament, and his collation remains a serviceable summary [Burton S. Easton, 'New Testament Ethical Lists', *Journal of Biblical Literature* 51 (1932)]. The lists are Mark 7:21–22; Romans 1:29–31; 1 Corinthians 5:9–11 and 6:9–10; 2 Corinthians 6:6–7; Galatians 5:19–23; Ephesians 4:31, 5:3–5 and 6:14–17; Philippians 4:8; Colossians 3:5, 3:8 & 3:12–14; 1 Timothy 1:9–10, 3:2–3, 6:4–5 and 6:11; 2 Timothy 3:2–4; Titus 1:7–8 & 3:1–2; James 3:17; 1 Peter 4:3; 2 Peter 1:5–8; Revelation 21:8 and 22:15.
7. Hill, *The How and Why of Love,* 117.

STILL DEADLY